Parables of the Market Partakers

In memory of my mother Arati Das whose inspired thinking leads me right

SUDIP KUMAR DAS

1st Edition June, 2019

Cover designed by Gourab Das

PARABLES OF THE MARKET PARTAKERS

Contents

Preface

This writing is by no means meant to be a text that defines almost everything, explains a few things and stumbles on its own creations. It is more of a work of fiction than of facts, meant to stir the imagination of the reader with its innovative thinking. The attempt here is to draw a rough contour to be filled out with thoughts of readers. In the process reactions such as chopping, changing and even outright rejection are likely but not unwelcome at all. It is not a product of elaborate research along dotted lines but outcome of pains taken to address to self the answers to a host of sticky questions felt too silly to ask in the open fora.

Selling books is associated with selling of ideas. The pleasure of having successfully communicated ideas to the reader leaves an author fulfilled. Even an unsuccessful communication is not a setback because it tells the author where he is lacking and gives him leads as to how he should go about addressing his own flaws. An author is usually a long-distance runner. How many laps he has to trudge along before he meets his satisfaction is as treacherous a guess as the weatherman's forecast can be failproof. One can hope though.

PARABLES OF THE MARKET PARTAKERS

Foreword

Economics is a subjective science, predicated on human behaviour. Unlike the physical sciences there are no fundamental laws in it that can be regarded as absolute, independent of human references and transcending human attempts to regulate working of the laws to human convenience. Spurt in production capacities aided by techno-communication makes it necessary to carve out Mass-Economics from Micro-Economics. Here focus is on Mass-Economics, mostly implying Mass-Economics where Economics is alluded.

In fact, Economics is an empirical science too in which hypotheses have had little role to play. It has an out and out bottom-up approach. Quantities and variables here are only those that can be determined in real-life.

In a radical departure from the staid, stale and sterile measurability of data, this writing toys with intelligent guess on plausible but truly imaginary data. This book has a theme that liberally employs such data-postulations, leading them logically to form hypotheses, knowing that a reasonable hypothesis - nothing but synthetic theory - is unputdownable.

Introduction of the hypotheses serves two purposes. One, it gives a greater incisiveness to views in the context of Economics and two, it would encourage people to innovate ways to compile such real-life data as assumed in making the hypotheses and on which the hypotheses are based.

The approach is largely futuristic but not absurd. The rapid advancement of technology might be the facilitator in bridging the gap between what is conjectural today and what would become a possibility at a not too later date. Statistical methods may bolster this process too. In other words, this book is about possibilities. Possibilities that would give Economics a firmer grip on predicting for the future. If crises such as Economic depression can be predicted with accuracy the system might be able to gear itself up and chart out a course for itself and earn greater credibility. With this end in mind trial with imaginary data in the form of DAP (Data Array Postulation) has been done to bring out inherent traits of Economics and revive Fairness - lost under rubbles of theory, jugglery and ruse - also. The approach is provocative, not comprehensive at all.

Capitalism likes stereotypes inasmuch as ideas – however contrived, inclement and mechanical they may be but laced with the lure of Money – are more easily percolated down the line if stereotypes are waiting at the receiving end of such dispensing.

Creating the stereotypes favourable for Capitalism's unstoppable march is a big task to which a large section of the Capitalist literati and think-tank are dedicated. A still larger and formidable machinery is at work to push the ideas further down the line. The machine rolls out people-types with very similar tastes, with set ends in life in which Money figures strongly and a penchant for enjoyment eschewing ascetic self-denial till the very last breath. The world is seeing a steady rise in the fraction of such people.

This book attempts to remove cobwebs of historical development to clear the view for a new look at basics of Economics. Dropping the historical baggage part gives Economics a lean frame on which the possibility of adding a plethora of ramifications opens up. This book does not plan to proceed further on these lines.

Desire – other than what is carnal – has its carrier in a form of Money that we may call Desire Money or D–Money. It basically extinguishes appetite. The other moiety of Money namely, Value Money or, V–Money is all about enhancement of the quality of life. It is different from D–Money in that it never gets depleted but goes on increasing endlessly like the entropy of physics. It is created simultaneously with generation of D–Money when production takes place – in equal measure replicating such generation – but unlike D–Money it does not get exhausted by consumption or deterioration of product to which it corresponds. Value, the quantity, embodies the quantum of dialectical transformation. Our focus in this book will be Value.

Preoccupation of Economics with the Market leaves many other cardinal aspects of the subject poorly attended. While there are very good reasons behind dwelling at length on Market but generating the impression that Market is life and life is Market is either hypocrisy in its pure form or, an exaggeration beyond normal limits or, escapism defying logic.

The question is how does poverty figure in the scheme of things marked by mad rush for Market supremacy. Again, what prospect lies ahead of the poor where the Market-dominated thinking-process rules with Rate ascendancy transcending sanity. Also, what treatment the subject of survival of the poor can expect to receive in a Capitalist world blinded by fixation on Growth sustenance. The fact is, the poor is an also-ran in the race or, perhaps more accurately, a non-starter. Poverty is a side-issue or a non-issue with extremely high nuisance value as the Capitalist would see it. They address themselves to the issue of poverty with utter reluctance since firstly, they need to maintain a façade of humanism and secondly, without buying power in the hands of the poor their own Market system would collapse. That the poor would die from starvation is of little consequence to them though. The poor do not own any products that factories manufacture and do not pose as sellers in the Market. Some of them sell their labour in enabling production at factories and in the process earn some buying power by spending which in the Market they barely survive.

Others produce food in tiny scale with their inhuman toils and drudgery but lose out to sharks in the form of Intermediaries who shut them out from Market participation. They perforce part with their product at ridiculously low Rates compared to the Rates at which such product actually reaches the table of the ultimate consumer.

So, stark obsession of Govt with Growth is far from being an expression of its intent to tackle poverty. To shift glare from its own lopsided core policy where poverty figures as a side issue if at all, Govt runs doles and schemes which are mere apologies for genuine concern for the poor.

The fact is, it is impossible to work out a political philosophy where Growth and fate of the poor weighs in equally and with which both these aspects are taken care of simultaneously and with matching vehemence. The self-centered personal-gain-oriented outlook of the Capitalist does not permit him to be a friend of the poor unless he wishes to plan his own downfall. Being competitive means sternly and heartlessly oblivious of the pains that his actions might be causing to millions.

Think-tank *idee fixe* regarding Rate comes from the fact that a 50% decline in Rate would wipe off 50% of entire gamut of value. Most alarmingly, the effect of this decline reaches out to value lying in storage of the Vehicle. Who would be the worst sufferer in the process if such an incident were to happen? The rich, of course. Similarly, a 50% rise in Rate would add 50% to whole of value including that lying in storage of the Vehicle. There again the question comes as to who would be the greatest gainer? The answer is obviously the rich. The rich can absorb the shock because they have plenty to spare. The middle-class cannot. The poor is immune from such threat as they own nothing. So, the Govt is actually for the rich. The irony that cannot escape notice is that in a democracy Govt comes to power on the strength of the poor mostly voting for them instead of others. It can be said that such Govt is a Govt by the poor. To settle this dichotomy, a third factor is brought into play. Who owns the Govt? Who else, but the democratic establishment! So, democracy embodies a curious cross between aspirations of the rich – the favoured children of Capitalism – and those of the poor who miss the blessings of Capitalism and dream of decent lives free from stifling poverty.

To those in the Capitalist mould, the world would be a much better place to live in if the poor accepted poverty as their fate. It would be nice and easy then for the rich and their Govt to push for tame acceptance by the poor of peanuts namely, democracy, religion and social harmony and forget aspiration to become equal.

People and Economics

```
                                      |- Unconcern for poor
Value is priority -<---- \     |      /->-- Palliatives
Power to Vested interests  \  |   /
                          \  \|  /
              Sham Democracy
          |
Outcrop of Economics ->-- |
                          |
              True Republic
              /  /   |  \
Basic problems targeted   /    |     \
Decent life for all is priority    |      People's power
          Unconcern for Value -<-|
```

Parables of the Market Partakers

CHAPTER ~ 1 ~

What fuels the economic motion

Think of rain. See it coming down hard on a large black umbrella. Huddled under the umbrella are two people taking pains to reach an understanding between them. They have a bag each in their possession. One of them has some item in his bag that he is willing to exchange partly with something else in the bag of the other. One such item can very well be chalk and the other cheese.

To start with, the seller of cheese might expect to get one hundred and twenty pieces of chalk in exchange of one kilogram of his cheese. On the other hand, the seller of chalk could wish to secure one kilogram of cheese by giving up only eighty pieces of his chalk. After prolonged haggling they settle for one kilogram of cheese against one hundred pieces of chalk.

The man selling cheese is the buyer of chalk at the same time and the seller of chalk is the buyer of cheese at the same time. For the sake of role clarity in the present discussion let us introduce a medium of exchange that both the men possess in sufficient quantities. Ratio of exchange gets replaced by two different rates of exchange for chalk and cheese, each tagged against the medium of exchange.

Unless chalk is exchanged indirectly against cheese with a medium of exchange coming in between it is non–economics. Else, it is an economic activity, the umbrella is Market and the medium is Money.

Let us suppose that, for one kilogram of cheese the seller of cheese expected to get at least M_s units of Money for giving up one kilogram of cheese while the seller of chalk expected to part with not more than M_b units of Money against getting one kilogram of cheese. Positioning of the deal rate of exchange M_d relative to M_s and M_b is indicator of the state of the Market, quantified by the term Telltale Ratio (T)

$$T = (M_s - M_d)/ (M_d - M_b).$$

In Normal state, defined by $M_s > M_d > M_b$, T is close to 1 provided rates are negotiable.

In Super–normal state, rate is pre–fixed. This makes both M_s and M_b equal to M_d and hence T is infinity.

In the Abnormal state, when M_d lies outside the range between M_s and M_b, T is negative, zero or infinity.

Importance of actual rate vis-a-vis expected rates

Super-normal   T = infinity

range : $M_s = M_d = M_b$

/

/

/

/

/

Telltale Ratio --------- Normal   T = 1

range : $M_s > M_d > M_b$

\

\

\

\   /---Hyper-inflation

\   /range : $M_d > M_s > M_b$

Abnormal -----------

T < zero   \

           \--- Deep-recession

range : $M_s > M_b > M_d$

If the value of T is much higher than 1 it could be because M_s is substantially larger than M_d that is, the rate seller is getting is nowhere nearly as high as his expectations. Else, it might be that M_b is quite close to M_d that is, buyer is getting the rate nearly as cheap as he had hoped for. Possibly, recession is not far away.

Conversely, if the value of T is positive but much lower than 1 it could be because M_s is quite close to M_d that is, the rate seller is getting is nearly as high as his expectations. Else, it might be that M_d is substantially higher than M_b that is buyer is getting the rate nowhere nearly as cheap as he had expected. It could be the start of an inflationary trend in the Market.

Value of T is zero when M_s is equal to M_d except where rates are fixed. It means that seller is able to command a rate at his will. Here negotiation is lopsided and loaded in favour of seller – an omen for high inflation.

Value of T can also be zero when M_b is equal to M_d except where rates are pre-fixed. It means that buyer is getting an item as cheap as he desires it to be. Here the negotiation is lopsided and heavily loaded in favour of the buyer. It could mean that recession is setting in.

There is a third person lurking in the shadows at a distance, making himself inconspicuous. He too has a bag. His bag neither has cheese nor chalk in it but only a cat, taking a quiet nap. The cat is a super-creature that can upset many a known sales equation. The cat is Super-Marketing embodied.

Product meets urges of the seller as well as that of the buyer. That is, when product changes hands through a sale transaction. When such transaction takes place not by mutual exchange of products on either side but through the medium of Money the transaction comes under the purview of cognizable economics. Market is the platform that actually or notionally facilitates such transactions of cognizable economics.

More important - how the ratio of exchange is fixed between the two sides. There is no Holy Book where it is laid down that one kilogram of cheese has to be exchanged with hundred pieces of chalk. Moreover, in practice, such ratio is ever changing from place to place, from time to time. Nor physics has a basal law to govern such exchange ratio. A clutch of extraneous factors - together called Demand - decides the issue.

Demand comes from potential buyer's wants of diverse kinds and the wants in turn create the urge to buy. Buying makes the core of economics. Unless the buyer buys, goods will lie unsold, pile up and gather dust. The producer will be discouraged from producing more and the seller will pack up. There are numerous measures to grab the potential buyer's attention.

The core of selling tactics

Seller's tactics

```
                        /--- basics ----- display fare
                       /
                      /
                     /
Goods type ------------ frills ------- create aura
                     \
                      \
                       \
                        \--- novelties --- present
                                           proposition
```

The selling–buying chemistry

Type of goods	Seller's initiative	Buyer's reaction
Basics	offering the buyer the goods	nonchalant
Frills	pampering the buyer in three phases	1curious 2interested 3attracted
Novelties	seducing the buyer with the aura of ease and glitz	1bedazzled 2charmed 3overwhelmed

Sellers of Frills concentrate on bewitching the buyer with all sorts of offers of self–gratification, often going to the extreme. Sellers of Novelties make optimal utilization of the latest advances in technology, communication and organization besides equal stress on the glamour quotient and convenience of shopping.

Seller's own adaptation to buyer's desires		

Type of goods	Buyer's desire	Selling approach
Basics	availability at all times	keep up supply
Frills	1 good quality 2 affordable 3 elegant	1 campaign 2 decoration 3 shop ambience
Novelties	1 high quality 2 tasteful 3 hassle-free	1 online 2 home delivery 3 shopping mall ambience

While at the core of the selling strategy of the Seller of Frills is the product with its larger than life image, the selling strategy of Seller of Novelties is just a proposition.

In terms of trading value, Novelties and Frills together far exceed the Basics.

Thus, apart from availability of the items in question, what determines the ratio of exchange is nothing more than the cumulative impact of the prevailing extraneous circumstances rather than individual merits of the respective items on sale under consideration, loosely termed as Demand. The term Demand hides more than it actually reveals. It is neither the impersonal entity that exists independent of human emotions nor quite the measurable quantity that would fit in equations amenable to mathematical treatment or figure as vividly in graphical projections.

Instead, Demand is very subjective. It is the urge to obtain a particular item from the Market in exchange for Money. More specifically, it is the relative urge among a host of urges – almost unlimited in number and variable or ever-growing according to affordability of Money – that an individual would carry in his mind. Clubbing urges to form an aggregate may not have the exactitude needed for analytical methods.

Inasmuch as Basics are minor contributors to overall Demand, we may see Demand as essentially a creation of motivated traders of various hues and dimensions.

Attributes of Demand

```
              /---- a subjective feeling
           /
         /
        /
      /
     /
Demand is ----------- a quasi-quantity
      \
        \
          \
            \
              \
                \---- not measurable but estimable
                      only through consumption
```

Demand, which had a key role in the propounding of economic theories by early exponents of Economics, was largely made up of Basics at that time. In the present-day context, Basics has only a minor contribution to make to Demand. It is not necessary that Frills and Novelties that increasingly dominate today's scenario would duly follow the pattern that Basics followed and maintain sanctity of the classical concepts. Hence, those theories need to be either changed or discarded.

Instead of exploring this aspect of Demand, we shall move over to the strategies adopted in selling. Strategy depends on the type of goods the seller has to sell. For Basics the strategy is rather straight-forward. We may simply call it Selling. For Frills the strategy id somewhat sophisticated with the Seller deliberately playing on the mind of the buyer. We may call it Marketing. For Novelties the strategy is highly sophisticated both in the presentation aspect as well as in the convenience aspect. This strategy is so thoroughly attuned to the needs of the buyer that it virtually creates a parallel Market for itself. We may call it Super-marketing.

The rationale behind viewing Demand as an outcrop of trading rather than as born out of genuine necessities lies in the fact that in these days of emerging Super-Marketing even genuine necessities of life are covered under gain-oriented manipulations of options and availabilities. As Super-marketing is essentially about creating space for oneself by outwitting and shutting out competitors ingeniously the buyer is only relevant to the extent of being the destination of goods. There is a marked shift in character of Demand. What used to be mainly buyer-dictated has turned into largely seller-designed. Buyers' inclinations, feelings and needs are of little consequence as they are mouldable.

With the change in implication of Demand at its rudiments the Economic theories in which the classical concept of Demand had a very substantial say felt the strains of change too much to bear with. It is time we took a more minute look at Demand to find out the changes in it and adapt the theories to such changes.

As we need to determine Demand in the present-day context, we introduce the **ADDIT** (**A**nalysis of **D**emand by **D**ata **I**magined and **T**abulated) hypothesis.

ADDIT-1 : Contours of Trading

```
                              /------  Super-marketing
                             /         Competition-centric
                            /          Parallel Market to kill rivalry
                   /------- managed
                  /           \
                 /             \
                /               \------  Marketing
    Trading matrix                       Attribute-centric
              \                          Campaign to attract buyer
               \
                \
                 \                /--  Selling
                  \              /     Product-centric
                   \            /Limited to own produce
                 \------- unmanaged
                            \
                             \--  Bartering
                                  Utility-centric
                              Limited to own needs
```

ADDIT-2: Trends in Trading over 200 years

```
                      /------  Super-marketing
                     /    AD    1818 1918 2018
                    /              0%    0%   50%
            /------- managed
           /          \
          /            \
         /              \------  Marketing
Trading matrix         AD    1818 1918 2018
         \                     40%   70%  35%
          \
           \
            \             /--  Selling
             \           / AD 1818 1918 2018
              \         /     40%   20%  10%
            \------- unmanaged
                        \
                         \
                          \--  Bartering
                     AD    1818 1918 2018
                           20%   10%   5%
```

Managed Trading is essentially the push by the seller while unmanaged trading is chiefly pull by the buyer. Bartering is a non-economic activity while Selling, although falling under economic activity, has only a small contribution to the gamut of all economic activities. What used to be 60% buyers' option 200 years back has now become 85% sellers' dictate at the present day. Accordingly, the nature of Demand needs to be seen through a prism that fits into the current day circumstances.

Rapid rise of Super-marketing with its vice-like grip on all-concerned related to the Market has made the two-centuries' old concept of Demand - in which pull by buyer exceeded push by seller - antiquated and inapt a tool for study of the present-day Market dynamics.

As such, the time has come to look for an alternative to replace Demand. We may call it Enticement -constituting Marketing and Super-marketing only, ignoring the minor role-play of unmanaged trading namely, Selling and Bartering. Enticement is the percentage of success achieved in making the buyer buy under varying conditions of availability and rate.

As example of Seduction one may cite the trading in military hardware across nations. Neighbouring Third-world countries buy military hardware from developed Capitalist countries either under duress or led by politicians greedy to hold on to political power endlessly who need to flaunt own achievement by indulging in showmanship in the display of arms, even as their countrymen are mired in abject poverty. These Capitalist countries have special Cells to extract acquiescence from them. Moreover, such Capitalist countries have specialists to see that hostilities in the form of cross-border skirmish – or even war – between neighbouring countries remain perpetually alive.

Unmanaged selling continues very much to this day, mostly on account of producer-sellers, only the monetary impact of it in the form of volume of trade has significantly reduced over the years. Let us place the total volume of global trades in spinach and car side by side. Spinach has remained much the same as it was 100 years back only its sale has increased because of rise in population. Technology has taken car much ahead in the same period. Volume of trade in car is much bigger than that of spinach today.

ADDIT-3: The colonnade of Prosperity

```
                    /------  Super-marketing
                   /    AD   1818 1918 2018
                  /         0%   0%   30%
         /------- contrived
        /          \
       /            \
      /              \------  Technology
Prosperity Drivers    AD   1818 1918 2018
    \                      10%  50%  30%
     \
      \
       \                  /-- Expectation
        \                / AD 1818 1918 2018
         \              /    20%  20%  20%
          \------- natural
                   \
                    \
                     \-- Population
                  AD    1818 1918 2018
                        70%  30%  20%
```

Yen (Seduction) is predicated on Prosperity Drivers and fails to sustain itself unless PDI attain Critical Mass.

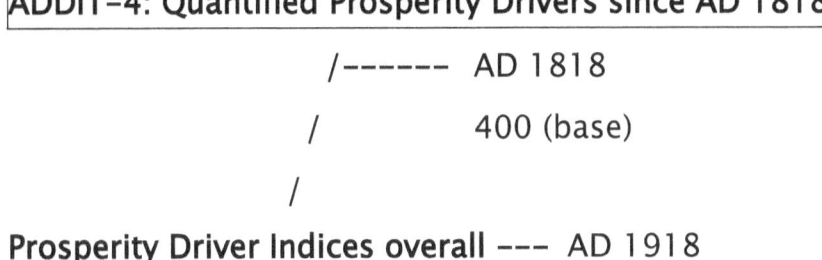

ADDIT-4: Quantified Prosperity Drivers since AD 1818

```
          /------ AD 1818
         /          400 (base)
        /
Prosperity Driver Indices overall --- AD 1918
(PDI)              \                    1,400
                    \
                     \------ AD 2018
                             6,700
```

We may assume Critical Mass of Prosperity to be 5,000 against a base of 400 for AD 1818. That makes Seduction a feasibility now. What this means is that the world is now qualitatively a quantum jump ahead of the world of AD 1818 and 1918 that we have left behind. There is not much difference between AD 1918 and 1918 in that during all those years Demand ruled the scenario. The pace at which technology is progressing it may not be too long before we see another quantum jump, making Seduction a thing of the past.

ADDIT–5: Growth map of key components of PDI

```
                          /------  | Super-marketing |
                       /      AD     1818  1918  2018
                      /             100    100   1000
              /--------- system related
             /              \
            /                \------- | Technology |
PDI                     AD    1818  1918  2018
           \                          100    500   2500
            \
             \                /-- | Expectation |
              \              / AD 1818  1918  2018
               \            /      100    500   2500
              \------- man related
                         \
                          \
                           \-- | Population |
                         AD    1818  1918  2018
                               100    300   700
```

Two factors mainly responsible for the quantum jump between AD 1918 to 2018 are introduction of the internet and the android mobile phone – both in the late twentieth century. It can be said that the present Millennium is different from the last one because of these two elements that have the widest reach into remote interior areas. Selling rediscovered itself by riding a three–horse cart driven by these two elements and technology. We are naming the cart Catenetics.

ADDIT–6: The Catenetics Revolution

```
    Internet Linking ------\
                            \
                             \
                                 ---- Catenetics
                             /
                             /
    mobile phone ------- /
    Android-enabled to
    capture Internet
```

Online marketing is the most vivid example of the power of Catenetics and its role as the new avatar and game-changer.

ADDIT-7: Key Initiators in Modern Goods Dispensing

Catenetics ---\
              \
                 Super-marketing
              /   \
           /   \
Selling ------/   \
                                      \
                        Modern Mass Economics
                                   /
Production ----\   /
                \   /
                 Super-production
                 /
Technology ----/

Demand is a composite quasi-quantity consisting of three kinds of wants – Urge, Wish and Yen in various and varying proportions. While Urge originates from genuine need, Lure is avoidable needs implanted in the buyer's mind through pampering. Yen goes one step further by shaping the buyer's mind in a way so that the buyer becomes favourably inclined to buy. That is, persuading the buyer to buy, often without regard to his genuine needs.

Economics comes to a grinding halt unless the buyer chooses to buy. Buyer's pull is complemented by seller's push to consummate a sale.

ADDIT-8: The Catenetics Revolution

Buyer's pull	Seller's push	Selling points
Urge	Offering buyer product	artless, no hype
Wish	Pampering buyer	with quality hype
Yen	Seducing buyer	with ease hype

ADDIT-9:

Changing complexion of Demand over 200 years

Intuitive wants

Urge -------------------- \

AD   1818 1918 2018   \
     80% 50% 20%   \
                       \
                        \
                         \
Induced wants   \

Wish ------------------------- Demand

AD   1818 1918 2018   /
     20% 50% 30%   /
                    /
                   /
Indulgent wants   /

Yen -------------------- /

AD   1818 1918 2018
     0%   0%   50%

Seduction sidelines the issues of poverty, unemployment and income disparity. It has its focus not in general welfare of people but in making the rich richer.

Emergence of Seduction as the critical factor in Market dynamics by pushing Demand into the shadows entails grievous consequences for the naïve producer-seller who persists with traditional unmanaged selling. To start with he gets only a miserably low rate for his products, barely adequate for his sustenance. He has no or inadequate social security that would cover the production expenses he incurs and that he would need to invoke in adverse circumstances like drought, flood or glut in the Market besides other natural calamities like cyclones, earthquakes or diseases of the plants or animals.

It is a rather sad reflection on events but in order to survive decently the seller as an individual has to be clever, self-centred and ruthless as well. Honest toil does not automatically bear fruit unless the toiler modulates himself and falls in line with the general trend of behavior.

Crucifixion of the naïve producer–seller's conscience

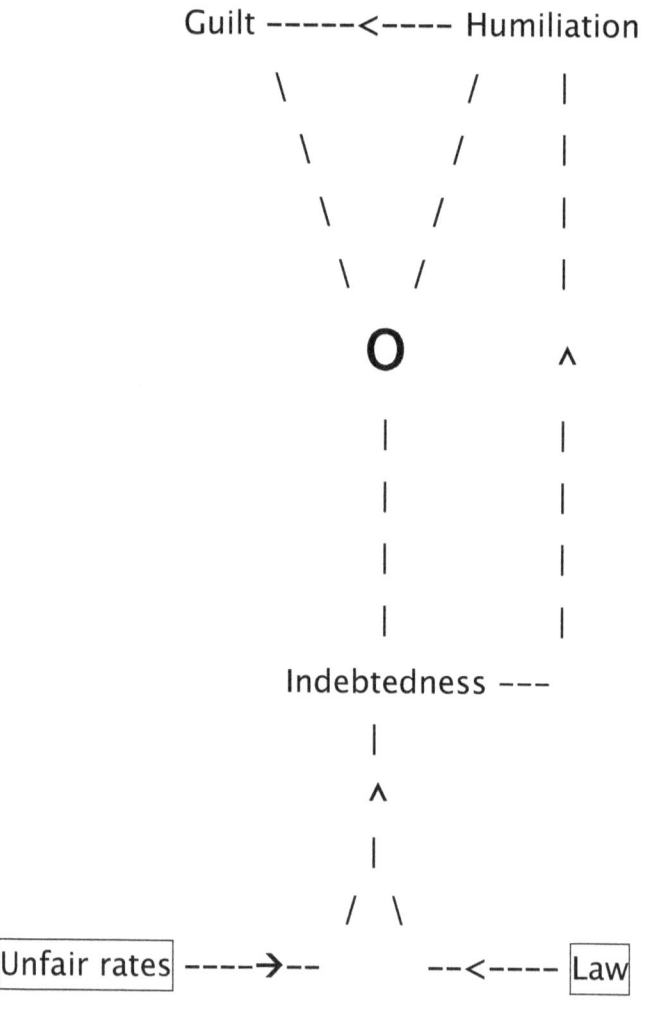

Guilt -----<---- Humiliation

Indebtedness is the primary assault on the conscience of a seller as it is the impartial view of the law that it takes regarding the seller as a person who, as a net outcome of his selling activity, falls short of meeting his monetary obligations to others because he is unable to get the fair rate for his product that the product might command if objective reasoning had prevailed. Indebtedness is a legally enforceable stigma.

Secondary assault comes by the way of fellow people. Branding by law lads to branding by society. The seller as person is humiliated by others living in the same society because he is unable to repay his debts.

Tertiary assault takes the form of self–infliction. The seller as a person loses his self–belief as he gets crucified by the law - paragon of fairness - and by the society - sanity enshrined in customs and traditions.

The question remains though that if this is fairness and that is sanity then how to define bigotry and insanity.

Under the circumstances, it is far easier to shrug the millstone of conscience off one's mind than adhere to traditional values only to suffer interminably. Unsurprisingly, that is the upcoming trend.

It is not entirely necessary that Mass Economics should be oblivious of the factors that make or mar the show that is Economics. The grandeur associated with Frills and Novelties may not be the reality at large. As such, crass display of elegance and comfort of convenience may place the selling strategies of Frills and Novelties out of tune with people's outlook on life. Once the initial euphoria is over such strategies may find themselves not so endearing as they used to be.

Managed selling is basically skillfully guiding buyers' minds into buying. In other words, it is an elaborate exercise in psycho-orientation of people at large who would generally be disinclined to get engaged in fanciful and expensive indulgences. Besides cars it applies to objects of art and it touches so many other areas of lifestyle. Mind shaping in fact strenuously points out the importance of you that even you had never known yourself before. It is subtle ego pampering and flattery of the most discreet kind.

Thus, there is an element of pretentiousness in mind shaping, the degree of which varies widely depending on the stake involved.

Parables of the Market Partakers

CHAPTER ~ 2 ~

How the perceptions travel

Economics, popularly a euphemism for the Capitalist System, is a contrived Agent of Time and a causal force, among others, of History. Any cause is an Agent of Time (AT) that, by acting under the aegis of Dialectical Materialism on matter, transforms it in a manner defined by (a)unidirectionality of change, (b)its shift to a state of greater adaptability to environment and (c)its elevation to a state of higher internal complexity. History is sum total of all such changes occurring over all time but involving man without exception. They do not unfold with *a priori* predictability but evolve as imponderables.

It can be safely surmised that the core of History is that part of it which is inseparably linked to Economics. The nexus is so intimate, so strong and so elementary that it is comparable to the umbilical cord. Rest of History is a beautified collection of characters, places and anecdotes to help give spatial form to the economic underlay of the period. A study of History without the underlying economic implications is very superficial to say the least. Every major event in History, including war, has an Economic cause of its own.

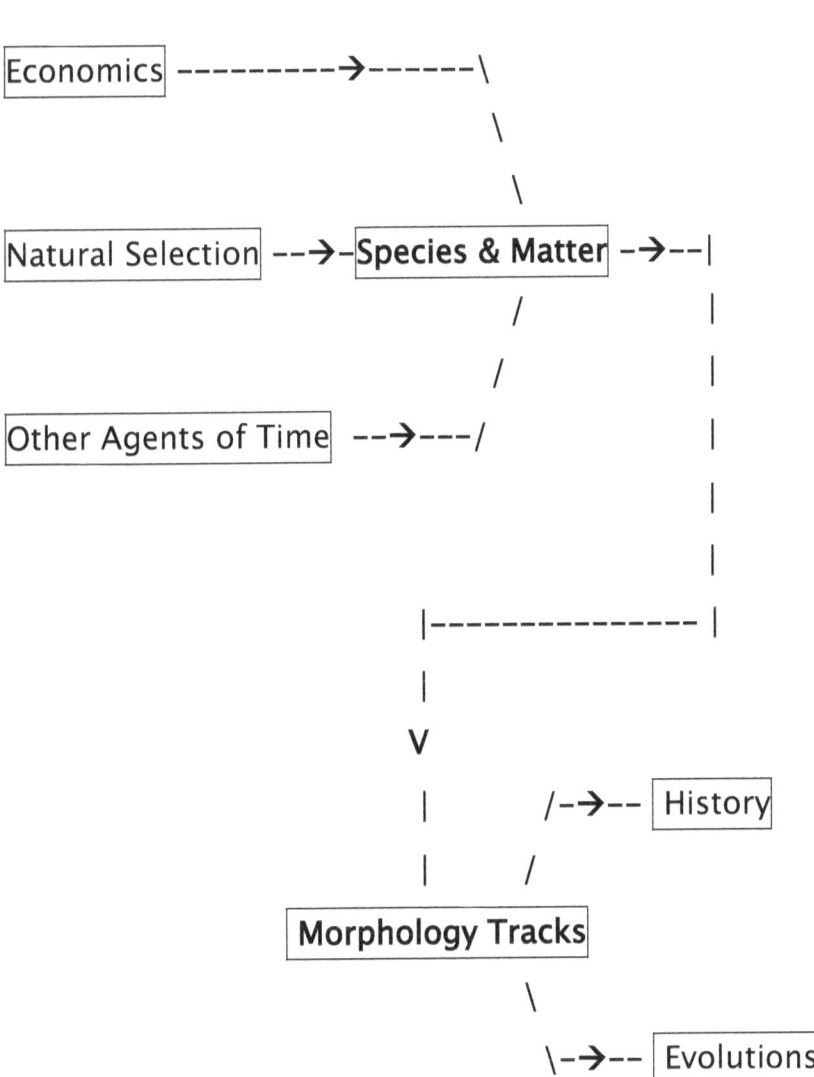

Perception is a faculty of the mind. Economics like other causal forces of History need to control mind, whose focus hovers among Spirituality, Sensuality and Equality.

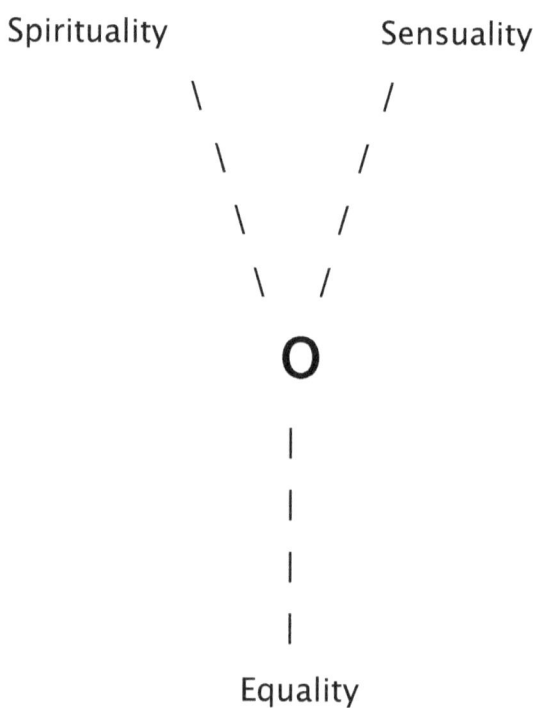

The Trifocal Man

Both **Spirituality** and **Sensuality** have the common property of Self-orientation while **Equality** is singularly attuned to Relation. Spirituality and Equality share the quality of Intensity of Belief but Sensuality dwells exclusively on Satiation.

Sensuality is the most sought-after attribute in men for practitioners of Economic pursuits. Stimulation of sensuality in people makes people more receptive to suggestions of participation in trade transactions. That means buying goods for consumption.

Spirituality, on the other hand, is indifferent to temptations. Thus, there is no point for a seller of goods to approach a saintly person with his fare unless he has some ulterior motives in mind.

Equality does not shun temptation but larger interests come first. The maxim is All or None. Individual desires are buried under the huge load of similitude. Commonality is not only colourless but it also prevents play of imaginative lure or mind-play. Nevertheless, it is an insurance for safe, decent and humane life sans the dog-eats-dog recipe of life under Capitalism.

Sensuality and Equality have the common attribute of Matter-Orientation while the idiosyncratic characteristic of Spirituality is Abstraction.

The Predilection Matrix

Self-orientation

/ \
/ \

Abstraction = **Spirituality** **Sensuality** = Satiation

\ /

Intensity of Belief Matter-orientation

\ /

Equality

||

Relation

The nascent mind of the urban child today is injected with heavy doses of a hormone concoction made up of dogmatic education, lurid advertisement and tainted literature to last lifelong with the aim to create adults whose mental processes survives somehow much like the lean subterranean stream in which the thoughts dwelling on equality lies completely crusted over by billions of tons of garbage coming from indoctrination, temptation and disconsolation. These are enough to completely overcast the mental firmament of a strapping young. In this all-pervading darkness he has to grope his way by following the call of the tune he has been made familiarized since his coming into this world. He does not have an option.

The idea of Equality comes as a distant beacon of light although embracing Equality is tantamount to going against the very strong tide of conventional thinking that social, religious and Economic fountainheads originate. He can survive but only by meekly going with the current which he does but in the process creates within himself the deadly split-personality. Equality remains man's long-haul destiny nevertheless.

Both Spirituality and Sensuality are contortions of the mind. The animal that emerged as man in pre-historic ages could do so because of several objective conditions coming into play. One among such prime conditions is community living. At the core of community living lies the spirit of togetherness through sharing. That is, Equality in the matter of distribution of resources. Conceptually, Equality would occupy the centre of common thought structure from which all other forms of mental processes would emanate radially. It is a journey with a clearly defined end.

Spirituality on the other hand occupies the centre of a whirlpool within the contours of the mind made up of imageries, vagueness and contradictions. The mind alienates itself from the reality of community living that enables the body to survive innumerable onslaughts to which it is vulnerable. It is self-deception invoked deliberately so as to defy the dictum of Equality.

Sensuality allows the body to overpower the mind. The individual is made unconscious of the benefits it draws from collective living. For him, own satiation is the greatest truth and central to existence.

Both Spirituality and Sensuality indirectly engender inequality by diverting the mind from its natural course towards Equality. Both are ruses conveniently used by vested interests with the intention of maintaining their dominance in a fabricated world order where inequality is perceived as the ultimate truth.

Spirituality thrives on Delusion – marked by self-deception and mind-insulation – is induced by self or imposers in which **God** is the Supreme Delusion. Sensuality runs on Illusion in which **Career**, the structural cog blown up with air of indulgence and steeped in molten nickel of ambition, is the Paramount Illusion. Equality has Common Station as the driving force in which **Equality** of status of every human being emerges as the Final Common Station.

The greatest misfortune of the modern man is that he is trifocal. That is, he has no real focus in life. Only those who successfully fight intellectual deception find their focus. Economics essentially deals with the vast majority of those unfortunates without focus.

When an economy is sufficiently mature, everything else responsible for smooth running of the economy falls in step but selling remains an increasingly unmanageable pain. In fact, it is the bane of an otherwise dreamlike scenario. Complexity in the urbane mind with no focus has much to do with the chaos called selling.

When a sufficiently large majority of world economies are sufficiently mature, production capacity in harness with technology becomes the supreme powerhouse. Since selling also involves human response to changes in product regime it becomes a daunting task, a consuming preoccupation, to sell – menacing too in dimension due to clash of interests. Problem with selling relates to every large–dimension issue in today's world, including war.

Because the urbane mind is trained to receive commands from trend-setters like the fashion designer it eases the task of selling when trend-setters get involved. The trend-setter has his limitations though beyond which his voice does not reach out. Yet the producer compulsively goes on producing more and more quantities – in the old trend and in wait for change of trend to happen – which do not sell beyond a point. Thus, growing volume of undisposed junks strewn around choking streets of progress is a familiar sight and unalienable from our advanced existence.

As our selling machinery turns out to be maladroit in the face of ever-increasing compulsion to sell, it is time we took a closer look at selling. First let us look at buying, the mirror-image of selling. Desire in the buyer's mind is the best opportunity for the seller to sell. A thinking man is not a good buyer. In a thinking man's mind desires get only chance of part-play.

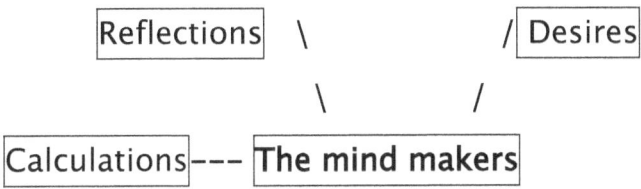

Logically, we should contemplate selling in the following lines.

> 1.Nature of **compulsion** that drives us to sell more and more.

> 2.Making **innovation** potent enough to ensure selling momenta.

> 3.Delving into buyer's **mind** to induce him to buy to aid selling.

Compulsion

[to Act in Opposition to Negative Propulsive Force (F)]

As our preoccupation with selling having reached a point nothing short of obsession, man is fast losing touch with the realization that life has many other dimensions that need to be endeared, nature's largesse being one of those, neglecting which would leave him a moron bereft of originality and soaked in abject mindlessness. This insane compulsion is a built-in feature of the capitalist system.

A' =   A

| Capital owning at start of cycle |

(−)B   (+)C

---------------   --------------------------

| Capital spent | | C_1 −   C |
| on   production| --------------------------
| ------------| | Capital regain| |Capital loss|
                       | by full sale | |to unsolds |

                       ------------- -----------

| Net Capital Retrieval by Product Disposal |

A' = A − B + C   [Actual Capital owning by ToC

                   (Turn of Cycle)

D = C_1 − B   [Maximum Capital Difference at ToC

E = A + D   [Extreme Capital reach over one Cycle

| F = C_2 + B   [Negative Propulsive Force on System |

G = 100 x (C − B)/A   [Growth Rate = 100 x [(A'/A) − 1]

Compulsion

[to Act in Opposition to Negative Propulsive Force (F)]

As our preoccupation with selling having reached a point nothing short of obsession, man is fast losing touch with the realization that life has many other dimensions that need to be endeared, nature's largesse being one of those, neglecting which would leave him a moron bereft of originality and soaked in abject mindlessness. This insane compulsion is a built-in feature of the capitalist system.

Obviously, minimization of F is most desirable. It can be achieved by a combination of minimized B and minimized C_2. When B is stable, as in a situation with no major technology changes, the focus is on C_2 that is, intensive selling to minimize unsalables.

Innovation (I)

As Capital enlarges, proportionate increase in sales becomes a dire necessity to prevent the negative propulsion force F from taking control and throw the economy in disarray.

Continuous system update through innovation is a powerful solution. It has a two-pronged approach one of which is to change technology to bring down production expenses and the other is to add to product dimensions with sale prices at par with existing products.

Hallucination (H)

Taste lives in the mind. Ultimately, sustainability of the system depends on the buyer's rejection. The buyer's buys in a scenario of vastly enlarged capitals are aimed at satisfying a wide spectrum of needs, mostly contrived, but also consisting of the basic needs. The contrivance at work is engineered by desperate sellers. If people are not credulous enough for the taste-makers to work on their minds the Capitalist system would come to a grinding halt. Ideally, one need not be too wise, have to be reasonably gullible and should be inclined to go with the tide. Till $I + H > F$, Capitalism survives.

Life expectancy profile of Capitalism may be represented in diagram as under.

```
                                    Innovation
                                       /
                                      /
Negative Propulsive Force----- Capitalism in Balance
                                      \
                                       \
                                   Hallucination
```

Parables of the Market Partakers

CHAPTER ~ 3 ~

Towards a better world?

Arguably, the order in Nature is that some lives are to be preyed upon by the preying. It does not mean at all that those preyed upon do not have a right to be alive. Betterment of the world must be guided by this spirit.

We live under the aegis of the Capitalist System (CS) but hardly care for an objective introspection to find out if our own vision of betterment of the world is in sync with that dished out by CS for our consumption?

The fact of the matter is that there is a sharp difference of opinion – we may also call it polarization – among people as to what betterment is or should be. Some people believe that betterment means the rich to become richer and the poor poorer. By far the larger number of people share the view that the concept of betterment must include the conditions of more decent lives and greater human rights besides narrowing down of the social and Economic disparity levels.

Most people do not do that for obvious reasons – the fear of being singled out for holding a discordant view on the issue. In spite of people's reluctance, we shall dwell on this aspect to find out what real betterment is and whether we are heading in the right direction.

If we regard CS as representative Economics then Economics is one among the innumerable Agents of Time. History is a measure of the evolution that occurred under the impact of many Agents of Time on matter involving the human race. As CS advances in time there is a widening of gulf between the direness of need to sell and the actual ability to sell until the gulf reaches the critical width when the gulf is no longer bridgeable making CS incapacitated and redundant. There, CS itself would change into a new avatar through the DM mechanism.

The new avatar of CS would be a quantum jump apart from the existing one with refreshed focus, renewed theme and realigned priorities. To advocates of Equality this could be a heady prospect as the chances of Equality getting a greater say in the formulation of the guiding principles of the new avatar may not be insignificant. It is a milepost far ahead of the present in course of our journey down the road of time though. It is a beacon of light in the engulfing despair for those contras who hope that human values will one day dominate the scenario where now CS with its own exigencies run a regime – overbearing but subtly so.

Now, let us examine how the CS, over the past 200 years when it came into existence, has changed if at all. A look at the comparative products characteristics of the two ages tells an interesting story.

Propagation modalities of the Capitalist System (CS)

```
                /---- | Innovation to Beat Competition |
               /
              /
|CS Aims| ------------- | Growth of Capital |
              \
               \
                \---- | Product Selection on Salability |
```

So, the decision on the items to be made originates in the selfish aims of the capitalist. It has little to do with the plight of man, his Needs and his priorities. That CS actually serves Needs of man is largely incidental and choice of Need Items as manufacturable is predicated on Need Items fulfilling selection criteria for products.

```
                    /-→--  Product Array Evolution
                   /
CS--→-- Man and Product
                   \
                    \-→--  Virtual Evolution of Psyche
```

It is really worthwhile to mull over the point that not all of our needs are our needs really. Many are imposed needs – fabricated and inlaid with attractiveness of a synthetic kind. What people do when they have lots of Money but few options for spending? They look for newer ways to spend and here the artificial needs come handy.

We may visualize through imagination what might have been the Perceived Utility Profile of Products (PUPP) in the year 1815 (CS-0), which we tentatively regard as the year when the Capitalist System came into existence. We put forward here another hypothesis – the PUPP hypothesis.

PUPP-1: Product Type Mix as DAP in CS-0

30%	20%	20%	20%	10%
Need	Luxury	Destructive	Productive	Reproductive

Productive Items (PI) are basically plant and machinery (P&M) that generate consumables. Reproductive Items RI are also P&M but differ from PI fundamentally in that RI are not consumables – they are equipped to propagate into more plant and machinery. Destructive Items (DI) are negative products – weapons such as nuclear arsenal – meant to threaten others into submission rather than for defence.

We may now examine the current Utility Profile of Products (UPP) in the year 2015 (CS–200).

PUPP–2: Product Type Mix as DAP in CS–200

10%	20%	20%	20%	30%
Need	Luxury	Destructive	Productive	Reproductive

Evidently, there is a switch in manufacturer's priorities from one end of the product spectrum to the other that is, from the Need Items (NI) to the Reproductive Items (RI) over the past 200 years.

RI, being the most lucrative contemporary choice, outshines others as the prime destination of attention of producers. This shift is not out of choice but out of compulsion as derived from the concept of machine producing more and multiple number of machines.

It has a flip side though. Higher rate of production of RI implies more P&M that can be justified only if the CS is sustainable at a much higher rate of production of PI which in turn translates to vastly enhanced rate of consumption of Non–Need Items (NNI). Sensibility quotient in this quest for unbridled growth of RI in an indefinite time frame rests on ability of CS to absorb endlessly.

We may also visualize Product as a behemoth, with Need and rest of the Items as its body parts, growing at furious speed. Unless CS is efficient enough it would probably end up getting devoured by the beast. Organs of the behemoth have very different rates of growth. Evolutionary impact of CS leaves its mark on Behemoth Morphology, changing it from NI–dominated to mainly RI–based.

It may be pertinent to warn those who ardently follow this course. Some items such as spaceships are not for human consumption but mostly are. A point will come when products such as nuclear weapons, spaceships and the like cannot meet the need to sell to survive.

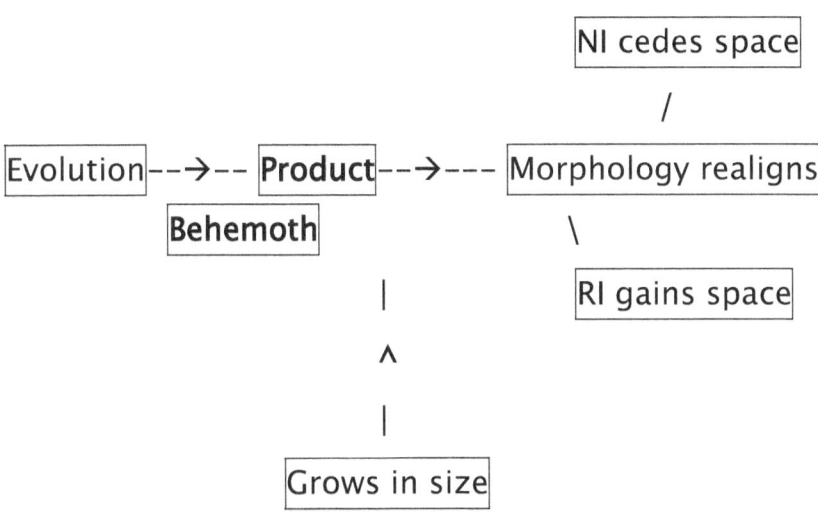

This in essence describes how evolution, coming from the action of CS – an Agent of Time (AT), has left its indelible mark on the most cardinal of the sustainer-variables of civilized life on this planet, the product, over the past 200 years. But CS, being an Artificial Agent of Time (AAT), is itself subject to Symvolution under the influence of an AT in a much wider frame of time. Thus, when CS ceases to deliver satisfactorily it may get replaced by some other contrived system with greater prowess to address relevant issues.

The diagram below ekes out how Symvolution works on Economy to put into shape the Morphology contours.

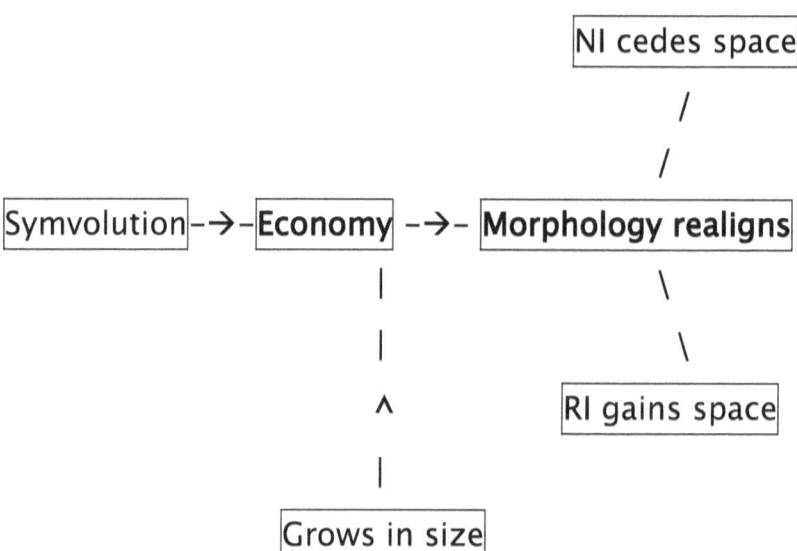

There is a producer, a seller, a buyer and a saver in everyone. We may call these elements the Traits of Epius. For children, housewives and other non-earners one or more of these elements may be missing but those are taken care of by the family head. For destitute people, notionally, the State is the provider while God, charity and benevolence have economic relevance too because of involvement of huge funds.

The Epius hypothesis

Epius is the Economic Personality of an Individual in Utilitarian Society.

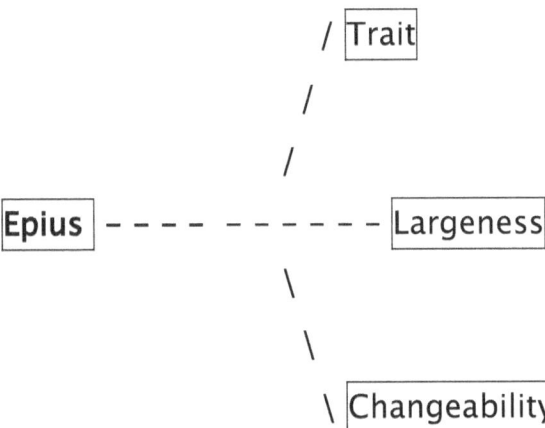

Dimensions of Epius

/ Trait

Epius – – – – – – – – – – Largeness

\ Changeability

Components of Epius–Trait

Producer   Seller

                    Consumer

Buyer   Saver

ETra (Epius–Trait) Data Array Postulation (DAP)

Individual Inclinations

[In %]	Producer	Seller	Buyer	Saver	Consumer
Trait–Ag	50	30	10	0	10
Trait–Bu	0	50	30	10	10
Trait–Co	0	0	50	30	20
Trait–De	0	0	0	50	50
Trait–En	50	20	10	10	10
	100	100	100	100	100

The various Traits in the ETra DAP namely, Trait-Ag, Trait-Bu, Trait-Co, Trait-De and Trait-En are actually major Trait groups as different from the social segment to an individual belongs. These are only representative, bringing out the relative inclinations of the individual with which the major Trait groups are formed.

Trait-Bu has the connotation of activities relating to buying which has a subtle difference with Trait-Co which is essentially to do with consumption. Within the peripheries of this section of the discussion buying implies pseudo-consumption that is, no consumption inasmuch as this is purchase with the objective of reprocessing or resale while real consumption means actual enjoyment of the goods.

While Trait-Bu has more to do with industrial, business and state purchases the Mass-Economics aspect is more concerned with Trait-Co that is, consumption of mass consumable articles. From this point of view, their focus should be on people of medium resources, closely followed by people of small resources.

Trait-De depicts the tendency to dwell on destitution as a lifestyle, either out of genuine Economic helplessness or incorrigible mindset or both. Destitution includes begging and living as parasites on other people's charity or under care of the State. It is considered as an economic activity too inasmuch as there are people – mostly well-heeled – who can not only afford money to help out distressed people but also take it as their solemn duty to do so. It may or may not have religious overtones but the upshot is that donations that are made and taken are too much substantial not to be regarded as an economic activity.

Let us now change our angle of vision in order to have a more comprehensive coverage of the issues. Instead of individual propensity we shift to the more mundane monetary aspects of purpose, magnitude and volume of expenditure at individual as well as mass level.

Here we introduce the concept of PeTra DAP which is associated with transactions and computed by aggregation of the outcomes of multiplication of each transaction with the transaction value followed by division by 2, as every transaction has two parties to it.

Resourced people's prime involvement matrix

PeTra Data Array Postulation (DAP)

(No of people doing transaction x Transaction value/

Nature of Transaction (NaT)

Degree of resource

[In %]	Giant	Large	Medium	Small	Nil	All
NaT–Ag	1	15	34	30	20	100
NaT–Bu	9	25	25	30	11	100
NaT–Co	15	15	30	30	10	100
NaT–De	25	15	5	5	50	100
NaT–En	50	30	6	5	9	100
	100	100	100	100	100	

What fraction of resources finds its way to what destinations is clearly delineated in the PeTra DAP, created entirely out of intelligent guess. It is purported to be an average of a large number of snapshots taken over wide range of place but within a limited time frame say, a calendar month.

Although the data in PeTra DAP have not been sourced from experiment it remains a useful guide in many ways nevertheless because it bases on accepted norms of human behavior which forms the rudiments of how any Economic transaction may shape up. It is concerned with deployment of money but does not go into the reasons why the money is being paid. It leaves us in the dark if the payment is to labour against work done, for something purchased, for some service rendered or simply donated without a recompense. It also fails to take into consideration non-monetary activities of immense import such as a housewife doing household chores or a mother bringing up children or a daughter tending her infirm parent. Unpaid social work also remains outside the scope of PeTra DAP. So does a thinking man's constructive thoughts which he does not care to put into money-earning channels.

Yet PeTra DAP can be very useful as a guide, particularly in matters relating to the Market since it rests chiefly on the money content of transactions. Economy is a confined space in which Money circulates with each transaction being one among a legion of micropores through which the money makes its way for becoming the circulation in their aggregate. Market prediction – a euphemism for Market study followed by crystallizing information from the data – can be very systematic with the help of PeTra DAP.

The first obvious application of PeTra DAP is for monitoring the change in trend. That is, if real–time PeTra DAP is constructed periodically and regularly – at least some sample survey type of activity is conducted towards that – any shift in spending habits of people would become evident. It throws up an early clue as to what people want now as compared to what they wanted before and gives the seller a chance to plan.

Now, back to Epius. Petra DAP can be a very handy accessory in taking care of the Changeability aspect of Epius. PeTra DAP also have in it the ingredients of the Largeness aspect.

The ETra DAP is essentially a statistical pictogram of the state of mind of people at large as to their mental make-up irrespective of the quantum of resources at their disposal or the socio-Economic class to which they belong. Periodical shift in the data elements of the ETra DAP would reveal which way perceptions are moving. It is important to note that ETra DAP does not bring out the reasons why people's perceptions are travelling in that particular direction though.

While Epius-Trait is the qualitative information on people's perceptions that gets translated into Money spending as quantified information appearing in PeTra DAP. The cause of course is rooted in human behavior and sharpened by stimulants such as Marketing, social pragmatism and technological advancement. Knowing how stimulants work one only needs to regulate the dose administration to obtain the optimum outcome much in the manner of a seasoned medical practitioner does on the subject of his profession. To this end, ETra and PeTra DAPs may serve as clinical assessment report of the patient's state of health, particularly the nature and extent of the malady and possibly its cure.

Parables of the Market Partakers

CHAPTER ~ 4 ~

The mind clubs

It is suggested that you look once into the mirror – standing right in front of it – head on. If you do not find yourself staring back at you will be surprised or even shocked. This is a mental conditioning that we cannot just shrug off. We are all conditioned – some way or other but certain basic conditionings are common to all.

Every one of us attunes oneself to the reality through the expectedness of the reaction to an action initiated by oneself.

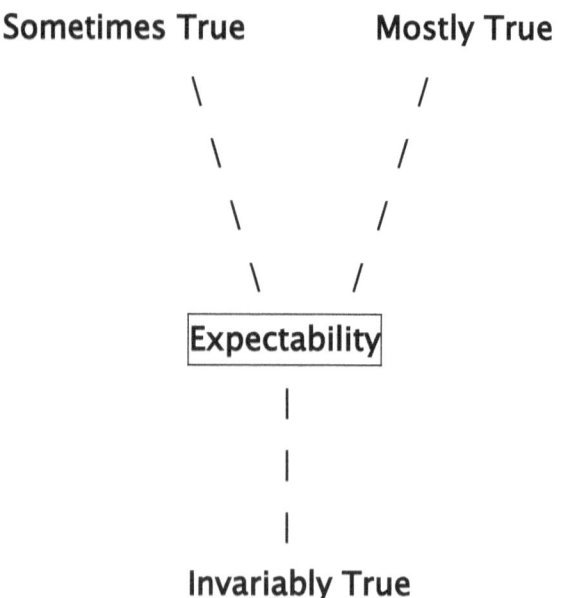

The basic and common-to-all conditionings are the result of Expectedness of the Invariably-True category. Generally, deviations from it occurs in case of misdirected perception caused by, among others, inebriation or mental disorientation or major changes in the objective conditions. Thus, an apple will fall ground-ward when the apple tree lets it go. A ball thrown upward will fall down. But in zero-gravity situations it will not. So, fulfilment of an Expectability norm is very much dependent on the co-ordinates of existence of the Expector or on manipulation of his senses by application of Weirdry-magic.

Some of the Expectability factors belong to the sub-category Sometimes-True. There is no problem with that so far as the Expector is concerned. There are heavy rains this season while there was drought last year. So, while raining in the rainy season is normal it is also not entirely unexpected if it does not rain at all.

Perception of an individual is the outcome of complex interplay among Mind, Matter, Time and Forces of Nature.

Actually, the problem lies with the Mostly-True segment. With a large majority of one's experiences telling one to expect a particular reaction against an action, one tends to put that in the Invariably–True category which in fact is not. Exceptions, although of much fewer occurrences, shake the Expector badly when it strikes because he had drawn up plans beforehand based on Invariably–True–ness of the Expectedness.

Our pockets are part of our Economic existences. That is, taking work and consumption of each human being as a unit, legions of which go into creating the cumulative totality called Economy through inescapable inter–relational activity among themselves, such inter–relational action is brought about, in many spheres, by means of material possessions called wealth and measured in terms of the quasi–material coinage called Money.

The Economy is a flattering magic mirror that creates weird images It makes the unbeautiful look stunning sometimes and the real pretty occasionally to appear terrible. Managed image can mask original ugliness.

It gives every human a status in return – not necessarily related to or in proportion of work and consumption associated with him. Some people try earnestly to reconcile Kaya and Chhaya in their lives and end up engulfed with Maya. Others – mostly mindless – keep Kaya separated from Chhaya in parallel existences.

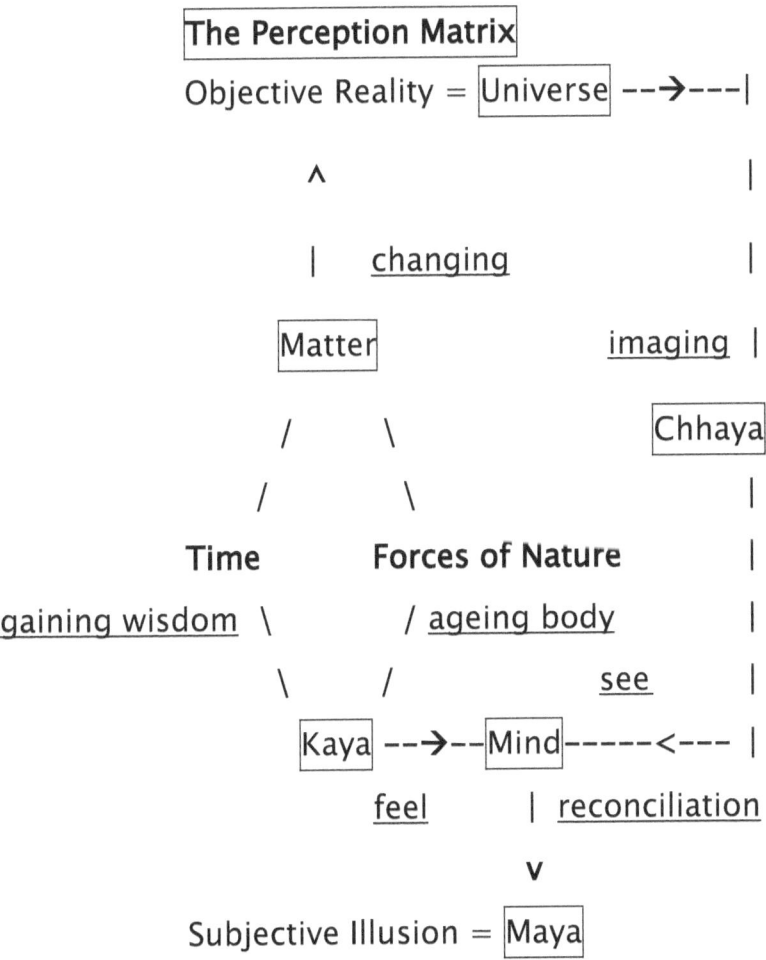

The Perception Matrix

Objective Reality = Universe --→---|

```
              ^                          |
              |  changing                |
           Matter              imaging   |
            /    \                     Chhaya
           /      \                       |
       Time      Forces of Nature         |
gaining wisdom \       / ageing body      |
             \     /           see        |
            Kaya --→--Mind-----<--- |
              feel        | reconciliation
                        v
      Subjective Illusion = Maya
```

Chhaya is the impression that the dynamic and changing universe leaves on the human mind.

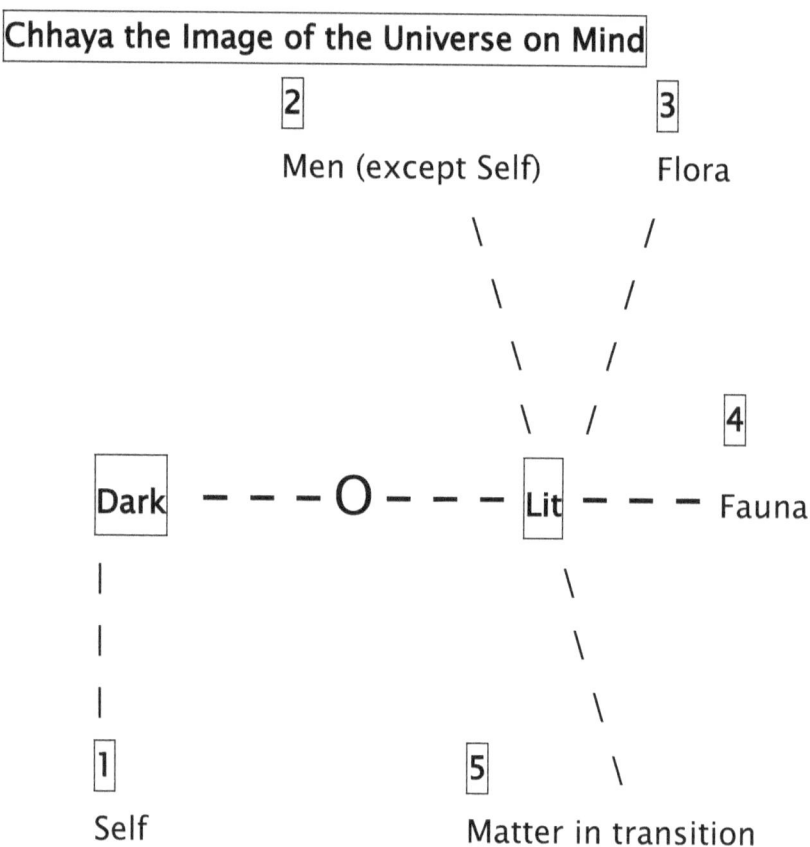

There is a working arrangement between Self on one side and each of the other four categories on the other. Manners, that is, relationship between Self and Men (except Self) is most crucial from Economic standpoint.

Manners is manifestation of personality through the range of Relationships Man maintains. All Relationship are the mirror image of traits. They are tributaries to the composite, complex and all-encompassing behavioural unit that personality is.

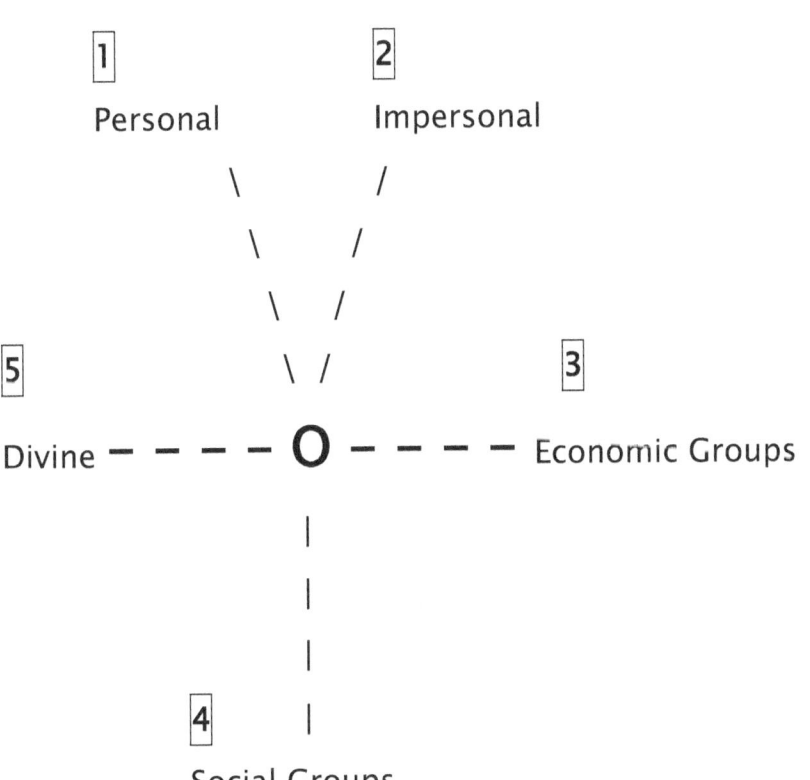

Manners as Reflected Sum Total of Relationships

Relationships are a compulsion, changeable with time. The way man conducts himself in his various relationships makes him a distinct individual.

There is a dichotomy in Personality too.

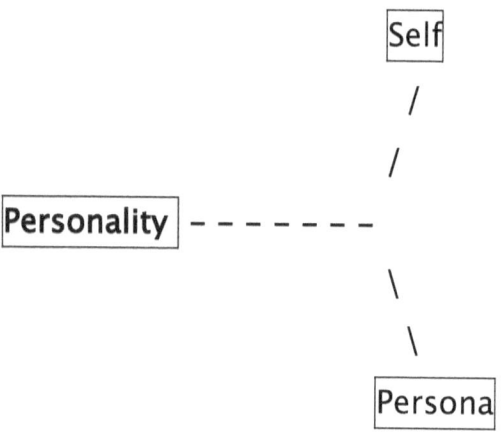

Self is enigmatic, inscrutable as well as invisible to others as it lives inside the person's being, has a very active role in the interactive participation process by means of which a person adjusts, adapts and synchronizes with his real and metaphysical surroundings. Persona is ostentatious.

Radii 1 and 2 in the Relationship Radii occur in one-to-one situations. Radii 3 and 4 link the person on one side with ensembles on the other. All these that is, Radii 1 to 4 are concerning humans only.

Radial 5 is an extrapolation of the reality into unreal abstruseness where the person interacts with a supposed supreme being as if that exists.

It is not possible for all five radii to coexist in a man, particularly Radii 3 and 5. This is so because Divine Relationship is imaginary and an imposition on the person's mind to induce the mind to be blind to Economic Group Relationship of which the person is a part, unwittingly or not. The more devout a person is the more likely it is that he detests being part of the Economic Group to which he belongs by accident or by design. This is Escapism. Someone who is deeply involved in his own Economic Group is a fake if he appears to be pious too. This is Dishonesty. Candour acknowledges Economic Group allegiance and behaves accordingly but neither Dishonesty nor Escapism is so.

Mannerism as Tilt in Composite Behaviour

Deliberately Eluding

Economic Group Awareness

|

Escapist

/

/

/

Mannerism – – – – – – – – – Candid

\ |

\   Rejecting Divinity

\

Sanctimonious

|

False Divinity with

Economic Group Awareness

Every person has an individual Tilt called Mannerism. Mannerism is a composition made of Relationship Radii in various percentages differing from person to person. Mannerism gives colour to the person's personality.

For any system dealing with large number of people motivating them to participate in tandem and to act in the desired manner is the most crucial factor for the survival and progress of the system. Capitalist System (CS) is no exception in this regard.

As such, exploiting people's penchants for its own benefit is the biggest task of CS which it pursues with single-minded devotion. No one knows the human mind better than the think-tank behind CS. Not only that, they have a few tricks up their sleeves to tweak the minds so as to make people behave in the manner they want them to.

We shall now dig a bit deeper into people's mind to find out how such stimuli work on the minds to bring them in line with their requirements.

Fate of its vast entourage consisting of almost the entire of humanity is inextricably linked with survival of CS. There is no ready viable alternative for survival of the distressed man in sight. As such, it is incumbent – albeit indirectly – on common man too, who form the great majority of Accessible Buyers (AB), to help sustain the existing system, however outrageous it is. He participates by buying religiously.

Yet, man resents being made a victim of circumstances, being created a moron out of himself and being invaded in the precinct reserved for his self where he nurtures his thoughts and feelings that bear the mark of his distinct personality. The Conscientious Desistor (CD) in distraught man occasionally raises its head, gives vent to impotent rage and helpless angst, voices disdain and dislike in defiance of moves that use mute AB. The conflict goes on.

Before we proceed with the narration of running battle and the divergence between AB and CD types and the ensuing equilibrium we take a brief diversion to dwell on the factors that govern the mindset of the unextraordinary types who make the vast majority.

Unextraordinary Mainstream Typical Mindset (UMTM)

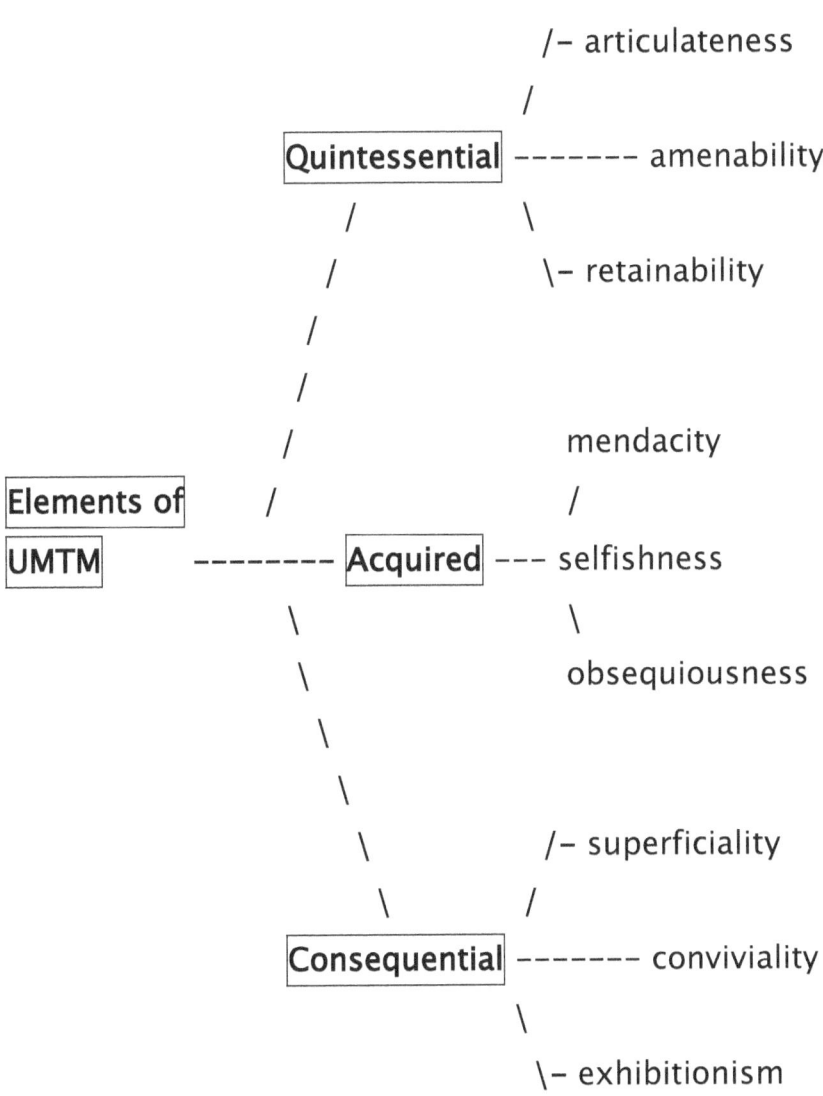

```
                                    /- articulateness
                                   /
                    Quintessential ------- amenability
                        /        \
                       /          \- retainability
                      /
                     /
                    /              mendacity
    Elements of    /                 /
    UMTM    -------- Acquired --- selfishness
                   \                 \
                    \                 obsequiousness
                     \
                      \
                       \            /- superficiality
                        \          /
                    Consequential ------- conviviality
                                   \
                                    \- exhibitionism
```

UMTM is a very valuable support to planners of approach in selling products. Each of the nine elements of UMTM is jealously guarded by the person belonging to the Capitalist fraternity. As such, any difference to be brought about in prevailing approach must avoid impinging on these elements. It is not only rare to see any Capitalist dictum making an exception to this maxim, particularly in the sub-area of Acquired UMTM. Instead the dicta often encourage people to be mendacious, selfish and obsequious even if indirectly.

Now, how does the system plan to deal with the trifocal man to modulate his views inexorably and permanently and bring him under the fold of the category in which AB is dominant and CD is subjugated? The obvious answer is to make him nearly unifocal, to mutate out the CD side, to shut out his conscience and turn him into a crusader of own causes, culmination of which lies in career. From selflessness to self-orientation – the measure of greatness in man has suffered a paradigm shift in the modern era. The AB man – a crude being – is projected as a cult personality as he is fittest for synergic survival in the artificial milieu of CS.

A prolonged run down the regime of Sensuality leaves its own stamp on character traits of man. Sensuality is a vehicle designed to transport man away from the inevitable feeling of triviality that comes with ordinary living and to transcend him through barriers of temptation – specially fabricated – to arrive at his destination of fulfillment where profuse sense of achievement awaits to overwhelm him. He is programmed to endear achievement and think little about happiness. Happiness remains elusive but he is content with achievement. He is hallucinated by fat salary, decorated posts and sights of imposing buildings, glitzy streets, cozy homes with delectable women/men/children – cutely attired and embellished – to accompany. He tries his utmost to run away from the seamy side of life. He is not ashamed to declare himself a follower of Jesus Christ but is non-caring about the happiness in pursuance of which Christ calmly embraced intense physical pain and sacrificed his life. What Christ contributed to man's internal civilization is not repeatable but can be emulated at least in some measure surely by one being responsible to society unlike the superficial and the hypocritical.

Man, under vicious sway of Sensuality, gets to show his career preoccupations as a convenient ruse for his shunning of responsibility to others in society and easily shrugs off the dual sentimental millstones of Spirituality and Equality. He buries his guilt deep within. He does not justify his own actions to himself and there is no one around to ask him to do that. Sensuality administered in steroidal doses right from early childhood makes him impervious to sensitivity that also lays the flagstones for the infant to develop into the AB man.

The reason why the AB man is projected as a role model is rather simple. He is the quintessence of the buyer who buys first then contemplates later, if at all. Buying is what keeps CS going. Without domination of the AB syndrome in the general personality of people CS juggernaut would fall on its face. Towards this end CS kicks ancient morality out of its sight and buries the raging concurrent concept of Equality under its feet. CS is as ruthless as it can be because otherwise its own survival would be at stake. For how long CS can keep up its selling momentum is a matter of conjecture.

Profile of the AB man looks similar to the diagram below.

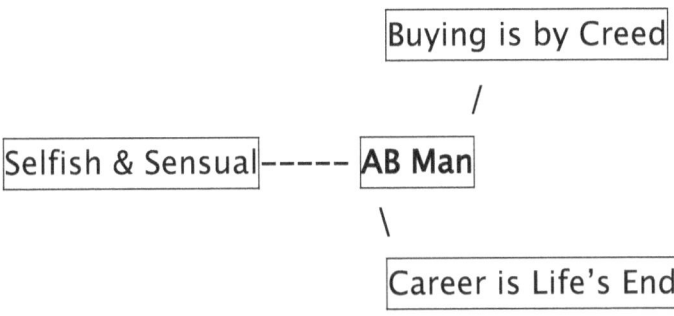

The most pertinent observation to be made here is that not only the highly talented people opt for a career to which his entire motivation is directed and in the process he might consciously give up many other pursuits and pleasures – a scientist for example – but in the CS dispensation the minnows also have careers of their own, often by resorting to dubious routes. This is a dilution of norms but serves the ends of CS as selfishness and sensuality is implanted in the fabric of AB personality who is a faithful adherent of CS and given to buying plenty because he knows CS gave him much more than he could have expected and deserved.

The CD man has instead the following traits in abundance that makes him a reprehensible being and a rebel in the capitalist system.

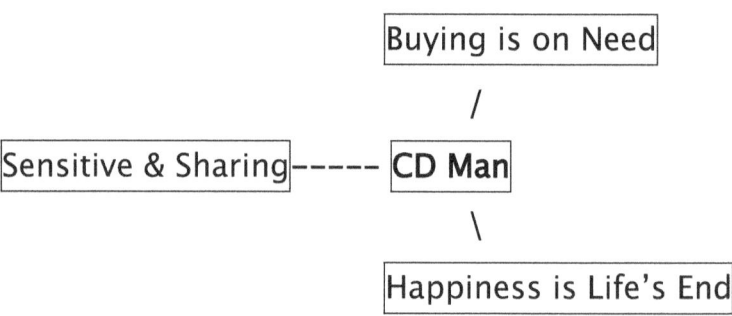

The CD man on the other hand is branded a rebel, a non-achiever and a pagan. He is subjected to relentless hounding, denigrated and ignored where giving recognition to talent is concerned. These are all done not out of hatred but for the dire necessity of sustaining CS. What all these lead to is a continuous and inexorable slide in human quality. As History advances the human fabric becomes coarser, weaker and more degenerated. But CS has a one-track mind that is exclusively oriented to self-preservation, not caring for the fact that CS is for man. That it is not the other way round remains for History to teach us.

As the AB man is a crucial appurtenance to the capitalist apparatus his image is one made of highly inflated glory. The CD man is painted as faceless, misguided, naive and pernicious. He languishes because he does not have the wherewithal in him to come out of the mire of ignominy and be counted. The ploy works only to an extent because the CD man is born naturally and cannot be wiped out entirely. The more the capitalist system tries the more it leaves the average mind in obfuscation rather than in conviction.

The purpose of the capitalist system is served though. A man without conviction lives on borrowed opinions. He is easily moulded as per demands of the situation. Even though he is only part AB man he fails to decide and goes for the default opinion.

It is appropriate that we should take a relook at Agents of Time (AoT). A unidirectional AoT is Entropy of Physics. An AoT for greater adaptability is Population Quality. An AoT that leads to higher form of complexity is Production Relations (PR) a contrived version of which is the Capitalist System (CS). All these AoTs work in line with the laws of Dialectical Materialism (DM).

Traits of Agents of Time (AOT)

Adds to Adaptability of Matter

/

/

/

Traits of AoT -- Spontaneous Unidirectionality

\

\

\

Adds to Complexity of Matter

The quintessential prodigal buyer – the AB man – is a prototype, an image and a creation of the CS meant to be implanted in human psyche to achieve its own ends. The net effect of CS, an AoT, acting on man's psyche with the intention of transforming his psyche unidirectionally to the AB psyche – the latter is endowed with greater external adaptability to CS and equipped with increased internal complexity to meet demand enhancement that comes with modernity – is that the psyche turns into virtual matter obeying DM laws. This particular aspect invites contradiction – between the imposed AB psyche, the thesis, and the innate CD psyche, the antithesis – that works out to an evolutionary process leading to a synthesis of the two whose culmination lies in the real–life prototype man.

This unrelenting contradiction gives the human mind under CS a mercurial turn. It can move unpredictably in any direction. In order to ensure that movement of human mind takes a desired direction CS systematically exploits the ingrained human weaknesses of fear, greed and ambition. Questions of propriety never seem to bother the exponents who are in charge of steering CS.

The fact that man cannot be tailored to possess a wholly AB psyche, however modern he becomes in course of time, has its own ramifications. One implication is that man cannot be given a single focus in life – against all attempts to transform him to unifocal he will remain a trifocal forever. Such an upshot poses a tough challenge to CS because the need for selling will only go higher and higher with further burgeoning of CS and selling will occupy positions of ever mounting imperativeness for sustainability of CS.

Thus, there is a real possibility of diminishing marginal effectiveness in transforming the CD mould to the AB mould. CS works in a mode where production goes on increasing exponentially needing more and more gluttonous minds to consume the products. Since it is difficult to transform diehard mental setups the thrust is on young minds. While it remains largely successful CS has to rely on statistical probability of whether a newborn will eventually grow into the AB type or it would foil all its efforts to become the CD type.

Parables of the Market Partakers

CHAPTER ~ 5 ~

Cycles, vehicles and receptacles of flux

Economics is dynamic as almost all things in Nature are. As such, Economics is best described as a phenomenon in terms of quantities that are variable with time and interactive among themselves rather than static petrification of realty bound by rigid rules working inside a rigid frame.

Factors that cause ongoing change to move in a particular direction are, primarily, production – being cyclic over time, secondarily, accumulation – in dynamic receptacles of quantified dominance by one over others occurring within human relations and exchanges – also called power – and tertiarily, perpetuation – of the power, endlessly over time, in a time–vehicle.

Production – whether agricultural or manufacturing – is cyclic. Agriculture is seasonal and harvesting takes place when the crop is mature. Manufacturing takes place in batches, matching with production capacity.

Cyclicality brings with it a compulsion – as product stocks get replenished at regular intervals product has to be consumed as speedily, or stock–piling becomes an issue bigger than production itself.

Think of a very large tank that has a fluid inlet and a fluid outlet working simultaneously. The inflow has its own speed, so has the outflow. Both are variable, depending on factors that control them. Generally, inflow has a faster rate than outflow resulting in net accumulation.

The hypothetical tank is a metaphoric representation of receptacle of running values where both consumption and replenishment go on simultaneously.

Let us now visualize hundreds of such tanks joined together by siphons. When there is very heavy accumulation because of fast inflow and relatively slow outflow the tank needs off-loading by means of tank-to-tank siphoning called exports. Contrarily, when accumulation dwindles, inflow is supplemented with siphoning in from other tanks – called imports.

An economy needs to export some products and also to import some others. This is a common feature across all different economies of the world.

Thus, both exports and imports are arms of a mechanism that brings about balance between production and consumption in an economy.

Production generates value. Stocks – the material facet of value – have a limited shelf–life and degenerates sooner or later. Hence, holding on to unconsumed stocks that one owns in the hope of carrying value indefinitely down into the future futile ab initio. Hence a parallel dematerialized form of value comes into existence. Since this parallel dematerialized form is immune from physical degeneration it is ideally suited for carrying down value without actually holding the stocks physically. For this, the owner of stocks has to exchange stocks with somebody for dematerialized value who possesses such dematerialized value.

This dematerialized form of value is Money – the vehicle of convenience for transporting the ever–growing corpus of value across phases of advancement of time and along the road of time. Money is a contrivance with timelessness which entire humanity agree as being the common form of ownership. The carried value that Money holds is not constant though. It is susceptible to variation and at a notional place called Market the value that money contains at any point of time is determined vis-à-vis current stocks. Here value content of Money fluctuates incessantly.

Since cycle, receptacle and vehicle all feature flux in the very core of their conception, their close relation to dialectical transformation of economy is a certainty.

The Economy in a flux

parallel store of intangible Value

Vehicle →--\
‎   \
‎   \
Dialectical elements of flux ---<-- Cycle

/ entry of fresh product

/

Receptacle --→-----/
store of tangible and transient product

Cycle ushers in fresh product, Receptacles holds the tangible product and passes part of it on for consumption. Some products like services are transient – they are not retainable in Receptacle – and are wholly consumed. Production creates product and parallelly creates intangible Value for storage in Vehicle followed by its propagation.

It is the Market that brings cycles, receptacles and vehicles together with functionalities represented by the players namely, sellers, who – we may assume for simplicity's sake – only have products to sale on one hand and buyers who only possess value in the form of Money on the other. In the process of harmonizing such disparate influences Market arrives at rate of exchange of every product against Money.

The Market in its simplest form

Sellers owning products only $\rightarrow$-\

        \

        \

        Market $\rightarrow$-- Rate

       /

       /

Buyers owning Money only $\rightarrow$- /

Rate is at the root of the process by which value supplementation takes place at the intervention of Market. It is the degree by which value is enhanced because of entry of new batch of product leading to cyclic enrichment of product stock.

Modalities of Flux

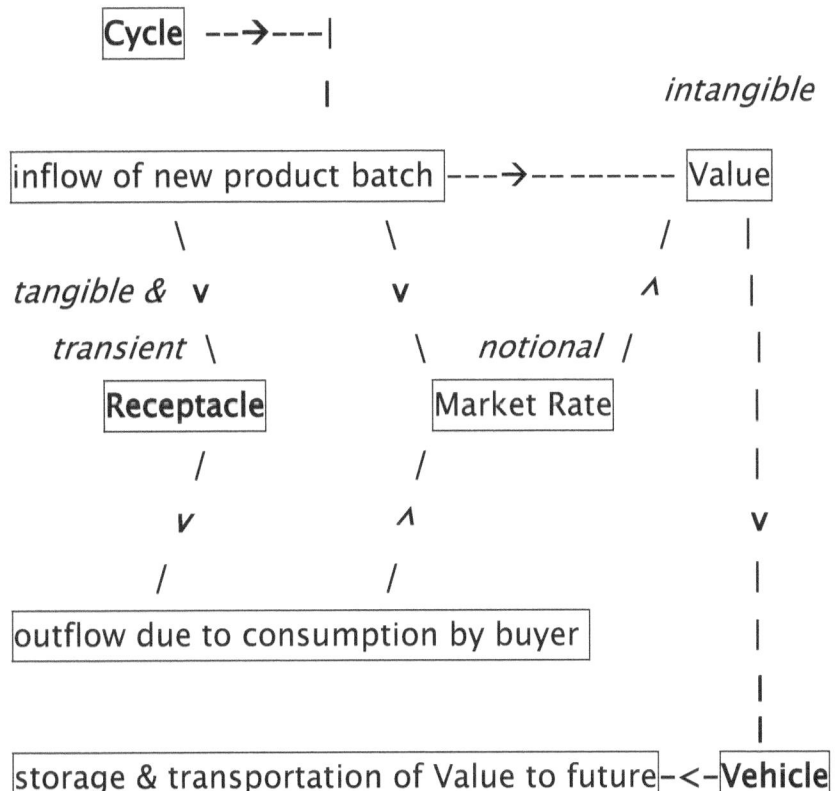

Thus, Rate determines the degree of supplementation that value receives from run of a cycle. Not only that, current rate impacts the entire value–store of Vehicle since ages. Rate, which is value of products against Money is also value of Money against products – in the immediate settings of the Market. A sharp drop in Rate that is, value of products against Money, implies sharp rise in value of Money – as held in store in vehicle – against products. This is the deflation situation which, though apparently beneficial, is fraught with danger of a different kind. Producers, who normally borrow Money from lenders such as banks and financial institutions, would suffer loss if suddenly after one year they find the Money they borrowed has increased in value relative to the current value of products in the Market. It translates into higher amount of repayment on their part. This could be a huge disincentive to producers and, if they are marginal survivors, could compel them to wind up their enterprises leading to unemployment and depletion of overall buying power.

Inflation, on the other hand, is beneficial to producers for the inverse reasons. It hurts buyers though. Hence, moderate inflation could lead to the right balance.

As such, loading the created value is culmination of a particular phase of flux which we may call Growth. Actually, Growth depends as much on volume of production as it does on Market Rate. Market Rate, in turn, relies on consumption propensity. Hence, Growth is a function of both production and consumption.

Variables that determine Growth

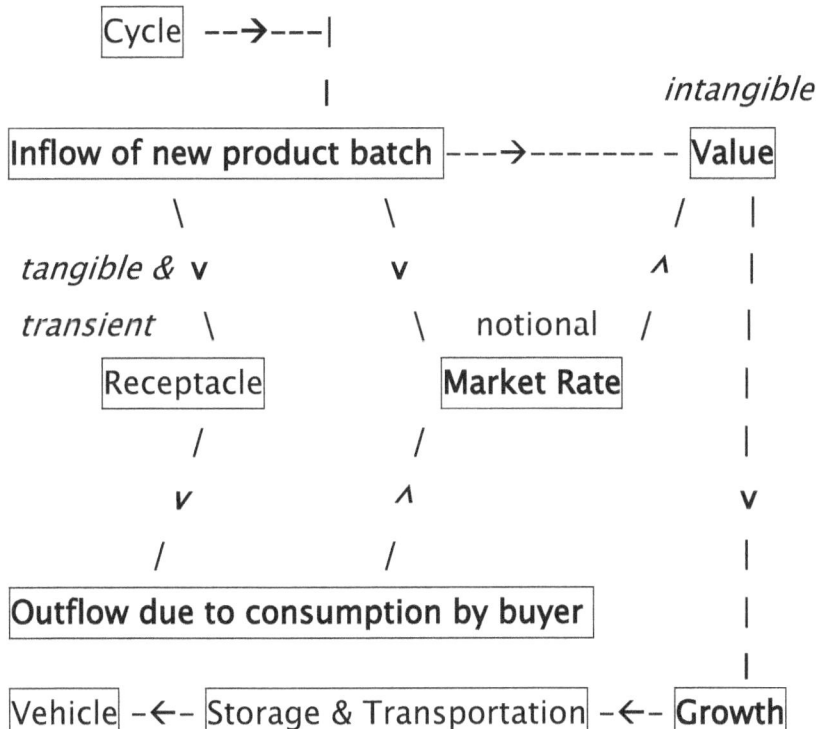

Rate can make or mar fortunes – made from the current cycle or accumulated from the past cycles residing inside the Vehicle – which is largely behind the crucial role of Market–play in everything concerning Economics.

Saleable items in the Market are not all generated through cyclic production operations. Infrastructure, Real state and Gold (IRG) are not only not produced cyclically but their near non–destructibility against consumption make it difficult to see them as products in the ordinary parlance. We can add qualifications to describe them as products with extremely slow speed of consumption – as in the case of infrastructure and real estate – and with infinitely slow speed of consumption as in the case of gold.

The prime feature of IRG is their ability to carry through endless or nearly endless incidence of cycles to give the impression that they may be regarded as some sort of store and vehicle of value. They are not. They do not have any value, only Money has. All they have is Potentiality of Conversion to Money (PoCoM). Among them, again, Gold is most readily convertible to Money.

```
                                    /-- Ephemeral
                                    /    (Entertainment)
                                    /
                        Fast -------- Express
                        /        \    (Energy)
                       /          \
                      /            \-- Rapid
                     /                 (Cooked food)
                    /
                   /              Swift (Medicine)
                  /                 /
  Product ------------ Moderate --- Easy (Clothing)
  Consumption    \                \
  Speed           \                Tardy (Durables)
                   \
                    \              /-- Enduring
                     \            /    (Infrastructure)
                      \          /
                       Slow ------- Imperceptible
                          \          (Real estate)
                           \
                            \-- Everlasting
                                (Gold)
```

Gold does not carry value across the time road. It carries PoCoM only. Even then, it is widely believed to be a Vehicle that stores and transports value.

Gold, a quasi-Vehicle

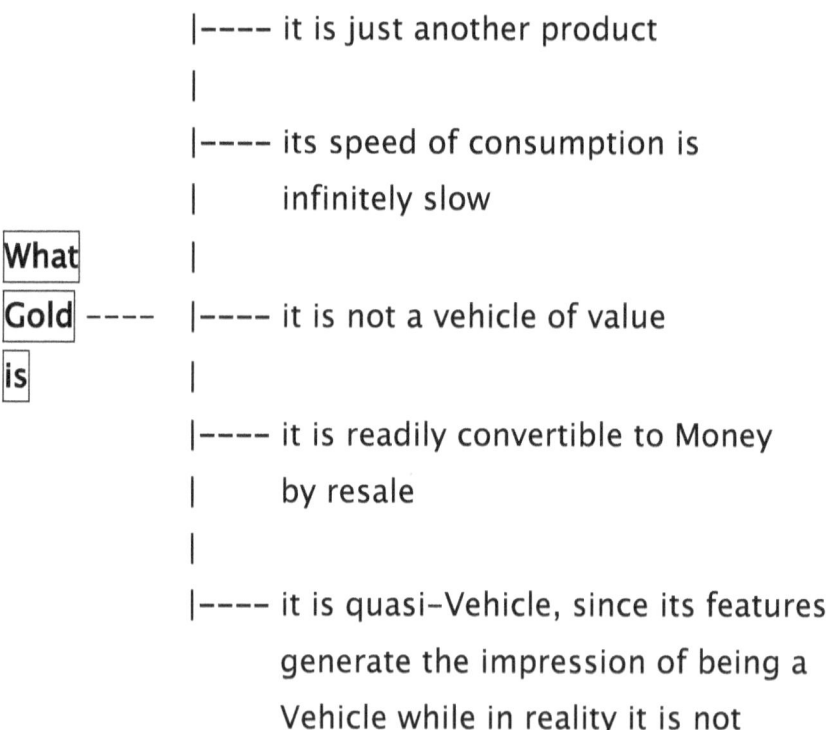

What Gold is ----
- |---- it is just another product
- |---- its speed of consumption is infinitely slow
- |---- it is not a vehicle of value
- |---- it is readily convertible to Money by resale
- |---- it is quasi-Vehicle, since its features generate the impression of being a Vehicle while in reality it is not

Let us look at situations where the General Index of Rates in Market (GIRM) fluctuates widely.

If GIRM drops suddenly and drastically, Rates of products against Money become substantially lower than what it was some time back. Let us call the Rate of Money against products as Wate. Applying inverse reasoning, Wate of Money against GIRM increases and the value store inflates. Rate of Gold in such a situation is more likely to decline than not. Hence, value and quasi-value not necessarily follow the same trajectory.

Even when in ancient times Gold was used as coins with embossment of some official image or symbol those were mere currencies and not the same as Money in the sense of the word we use in modern times. Currency originated at the royal exchequer while Money has its source in the productive toils of people. Currency – either made of Gold or of paper – is tangible while Money is an abstraction and is intangible as well. Only Money assumes the bodily shape of currency when participating in Market transactions. Money also borrows the name of the unit with which currency is described. If currency is the body then Money is its soul. Market cross-currents are all about soul-play.

To build buffer against Flux man opts to

```
                                    /--- Livelihood
                                   /
                          Product ---- Exploitation
                          /     \
                    from /       \--- Consumption
                natural /
                   urge /
                       /
                       /              Enhancement
                      / to save surplus    /
     Acquire ---------------------- Value --- Retention
              \                        \
               \                        Propagation
          out of\
           panic \
                  \
                   \         /--- Exhibition
                    \   /
                     Gold ---- Indestructability
                      \
                       \--- Security
```

Flux is the way of Nature. As such Flux is the way of life of all. Flux brings in uncertainty. The human mind, predictably, reacts and gears up in three different ways to neutralize, or at least cushion the effects of the uncertainty associated with Flux.

How Flux drives the mind in the use of resources

```
                    Instinctive --- meet basic needs
                       /                  (products)
                      /
Human                /
Reaction to  --- Intuitive -- hold on to savings
Flux            \                physically (Gold)
                 \
                  \
                Informed --- consolidate surplus
                               notionally (Money)
```

Non-currency dimension of Money is essentially to deal with uncertainties of Flux. The currency part of Money takes care of purchase transactions in the Market.

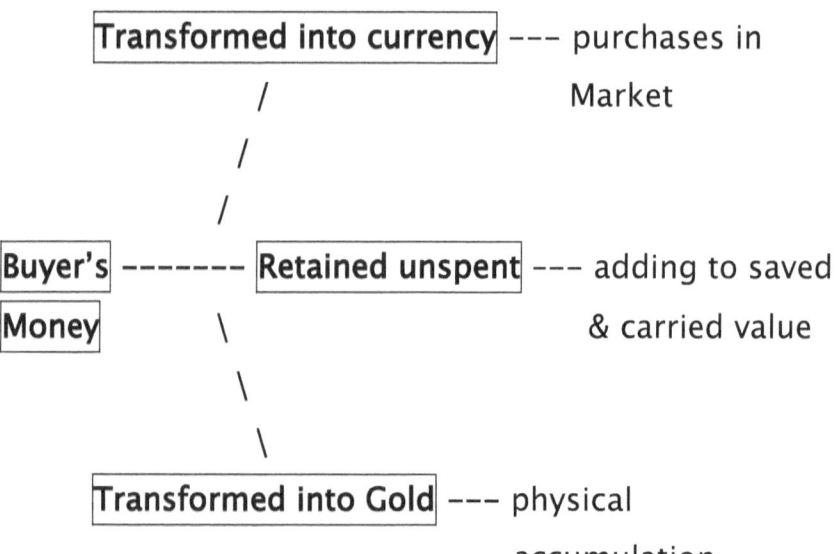

Modes of disposal of buyer's Money

Transformed into currency --- purchases in
    /   Market
   /
  /
Buyer's ------- **Retained unspent** --- adding to saved
Money   \   & carried value
              \
            \
Transformed into Gold --- physical
                              accumulation

Prima facie, it would appear that cheaper product would enhance the Wate of Money against product which in turn would enhance the value store. That is, inflation could be the most undesirable element in framing objectives. The reality is different.

Let us assume that there is a single product currently in the Market selling at the Rate of R and Wate W. If D is Desire Money (D–Money) represented by currency in circulation and aggregate bank deposits, V, Value (V–Money) of the current product, is

$$D = V / W = V . R / R_c \quad [R_c \text{ is constant.}$$

When Rates are stable, D–Money (D) equals Aggregate Buying Power (ABP) (B), but that is hardly possible in an inflationary situation. If D_0 is the previous ABP, D the current ABP, B_d drop in ABP due to inflation then,

$$B_d = D - D_0 = (Q - Q_0) / D_0.$$

D_s, Booster Buying Power (BBP), is cash injected in small doses by Central Bank (CB) to arrest rise of unsold stocks. As D_s always approaches B_d being less than it, a Hiatus ($H = B_d - D_s$) and its rate of change, Torque ($T = H_a /t$) (H_a is average Hiatus, t is time), persists. Under inflation T invariably makes stocks pile up, despite BBP.

Immediate effect of this move by CB is three-fold. Existing idle D-Money holders are affected adversely by inflation – since their buying power drops from B_0 to B – injection of liquidity does not address this aspect. As Rate is higher Money becomes cheaper that is, $W < W_0$. As such, inflation is beneficial to people engaged in production since firstly, inflation fetches good revenue and secondly, with Money cheaper they pay less on loans they made for production earlier. It makes no sense to the poor as rates remain same.

So, inflation gives rise to a conflict of interests between groups – one, those already holding D-Money who are made to suffer, two, those engaged in the process of creating D-Money who rejoice and three those who neither hold D-Money nor produce it but who buy essential items in the Market against earnings made with their labour. The last named are the poor who suffer most from the impact of inflation.

Thus, inflation is a menace. Since more production gives more Buying Power to buyers that could make products affordable even as they get costlier, there is a tendency among the think-tank to encourage production even in inflationary situations.

Forms of Money by usage

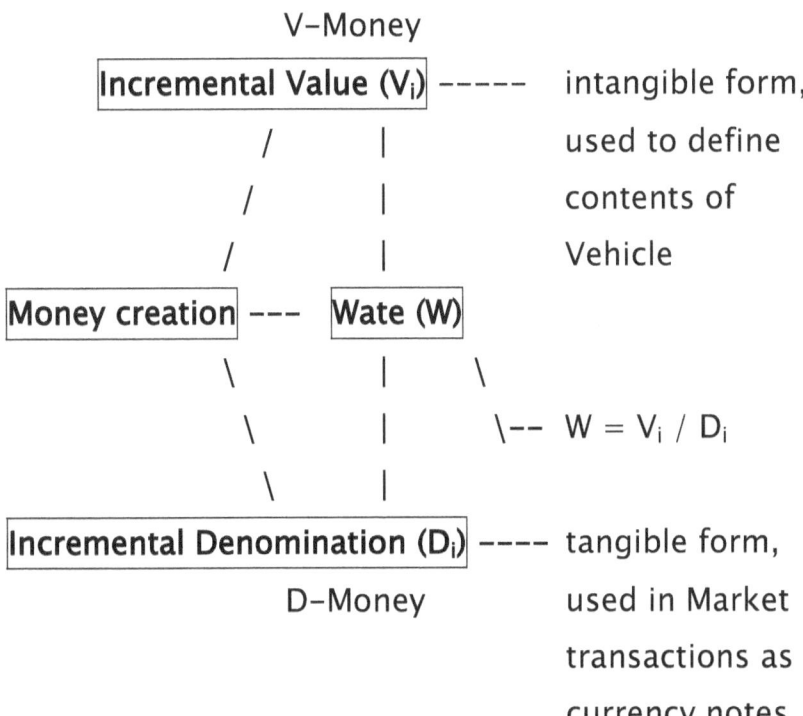

A relieving antidote cannot be cure for chronic illness. *A cat chasing its own tail may, by an extraordinary act of feline dexterity, succeed on occasion in catching it. To overcome inflation by increasing production, while superficially similar, will not so often be successful*[1].

1 J. K. Galbraith : The Affluent Society (Penguin Books 1999) p.158

Money occurring as Denomination is measurable since volume of currency in circulation is known to the Issuing Authority and information on aggregate of balances lying in Bank Accounts is also available. There is no other contributory to D–Money.

Money retained over ages as Value cannot be measured. It can only be estimated through application of intelligent guess. Such a guesswork cannot quite be accurate.

As such, what impact inflation leaves on an economy is as difficult to find out with any degree of accuracy as it would be to make forecasts base on that because inflation has a close and direct bearing on the gamut of value in the economy. The problem lies essentially in the fact that Value is an intangible quantity.

Incidentally, Gold, Real estate, investment etc possess no Value but are merely products which are convertible to D–Money by resale. That the resale proceeds are quite substantial even after prolonged use does not earn them the recognition as a form of Money that Value is. As such, they do not enter the calculation of Value.

Spectrum of Money users

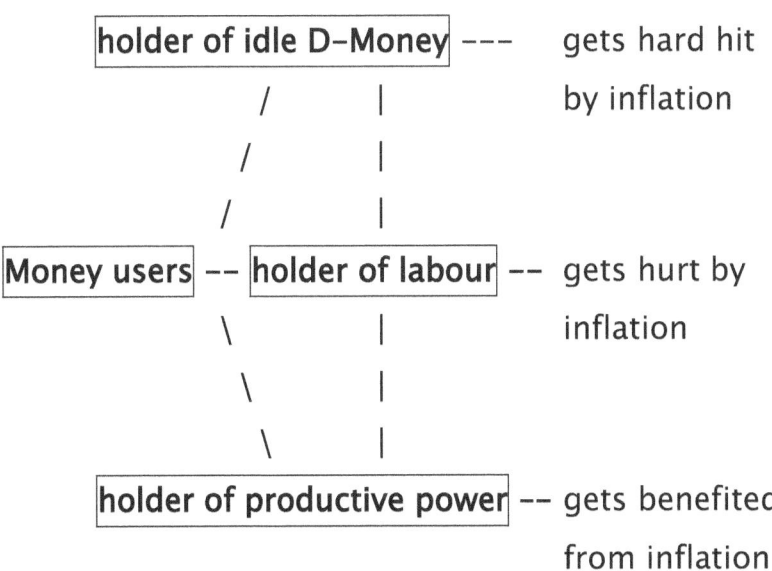

holder of idle D-Money --- gets hard hit
by inflation

Money users -- holder of labour -- gets hurt by
inflation

holder of productive power -- gets benefited
from inflation

Inflation is the order of the day as the producers' lobby everywhere have wrested political power. In sync with fear of Deflation-spiral havoc of 1929-35 it has a vice-like grip on thinking. Inflation has its strong sides too as it encourages production which in turn creates more employment and buying power.

D-Money may get partially used up by consumption, degradation, obsolescence of tangible product or may be fully utilized against transient product. V-Money is indestructible. Once created, it lasts forever.

Based on quantum of production, Central Bank of the country prints currency notes to release additional D-Money into the economy, which normally gravitates towards (1) enhancement of rate of idle products such as Gold and real estate by their resale (2) enhancement of rates of shares by resale (3) imports – mainly of machinery, technology and luxury items (4) meeting Govt expenses shortfall in the form of budget deficit.

Printing currency notes supplements revenue earnings of Govt and allows it to spend more. If such additional Govt spending is towards boosting infrastructure, it gives a fillip to production. Else, if such Govt spending merely goes to hike salary of Govt employees as a populist measure and political expedient it can create a backlash in the form of steep increase in inflation unless the economy is growing at a fast pace. The reason is – with the same quantum of products available in the Market, larger volume of cash in the hands of buyers would kick up the Market rates.

Flux : achievable(+) and undesirable(–) ends

```
                    tangible accrual ---- D-Money
                        /     buying power(+) disparity(-)
                       /
        production --- incidental accrual --- Class
            /     \            barrier(-) struggle(-)
           /       \
          /         intangible accrual ---- V-Money
         /                          quality of life(+)
        /
  Flux modes
       \
        \           tiny group ------ family
         \              /         love(+) bond(+)
          \           /
      human relation --- big group --- community
              \                  harmony(+) envy(-)
               \
              large group ----- society
                          equality(+) obscurantism(-)
```

Surfeit of liquidity in the economy through injection of currency notes printed in unrestrained manner can be a sure recipe for recession if such injection is not for infrastructure development but for raising salaries in cushy jobs and not matched by rise in production. If production is static or on the decline as may happen when manufactured items become non-competitive against similar imported items, buying power in the hands of ordinary people who make their income from selling their labour would dwindle as an immediate consequence, high salaries of the privileged few notwithstanding. In such circumstances people with limited buying power would opt for cheaper imported varieties leaving the local costlier product unsold. Indigenous producers of such unsold products would wind up business sooner or later, causing further decline in buying power in a spiral.

The volume of fresh printing of currency notes must at least be equal to quantum of production. Alternative to printing is slackening of the rate of compulsory reserve of banks with the Central Bank. Else, there would be excess product in the Market and not enough cash to buy those. This is a perfect setting for deflation which the policy framers would avoid by all means.

Relative Rates of products *inter se* have a far-reaching consequence. *In a world of scarcity, choosing one thing means giving up something else. The opportunity cost of a decision is the value of the good or service foregone[2].* The choices chalk out the course D-Money would take and in what channels V-Money would flow. Rate structure induces choice that in turn helps fill in the matrix of what percentage of D-Money goes to which area of product by relative preferences. V-Money replicates the pattern. Thus, Rate fixing – the overtly innocuous game of discretion – is the key to dialectical path-setting – notwithstanding lackadaisical approach of Sellers, manipulative practices of Marketeers and moulding of Market with creation of parallel Markets by Super-marketeers. Actually, these traits get factored in in the formation of Value.

Attempts to boost mass buying power through large-scale and indiscriminate lending of personal loans or housing loans would fail to lift the level of production since people with enhanced buying power would still go for the cheaper imports. Moreover, in trying to be competitive cheap labour is outsourced from other countries – hitting jobs and buying power.

2 P. A. Samuelson & W. D. Nordhaus : Economics 19th edition, p.17

Fixing inflation at the optimum level is as hard a task faced by economic policy planners as determining what is optimum. In a democratic country like India where around 80% of the populace is desperately poor, controlling inflation is an issue of very big dimension and very wide ramifications.

The Receptacle contains product that has been created by the cycle just concluded plus accumulation of left overs of previous cycles. Value, although an intangible quantity, its incremental growth can be quantified by linking it to corresponding physical product. Taking Q as Quantum of production

$$V = Q . R \quad \text{[R is prevalent Market Rate.}$$

Value, a form of Money, can neither be directly converted to Denomination – the other form of Money – nor can be employed for direct and immediate gains elsewhere. Yet it works wonder, albeit indirectly, on sustenance of life, preservation of Nature, security, knowledge, education, skill, quality of life, quality of system organization – in factory, hospital, hotel etc – and research – academic, medical, technological etc. These Values impact efficiency of production and product quality tremendously besides improving life.

Parables of the Market Partakers

CHAPTER ~ 6 ~

Lay pigeons, clay pigeons

Those familiar with the card game of contract bridge knows very well how not to allow the appearance in active play of a particular game–changer card in the hands of the opponents that in all probability would ruin their own game. The idea is to preempt play of that card through clever ploys like trumping it out or forcing it to be dumped during non–suit handplay. Niceties of contract bridge is merely a simile for a more mundane but immensely more prosaic, pathetic and poignant aspect of life which we are now to discuss.

A question of life that probably remains uppermost in the minds of by far the vast majority of people over forgotten length of years, centuries and millennia is very easy to ask but immeasurably difficult to answer to which we may take a look now. That is, we shall examine what is the difficulty – if it is at all difficult – that elevates it to the level of ones concerning existence of God or physical organization within the living beings and rest of the universe.

The poser is : "Are the minnows – the poor, hapless and downtrodden people of the world – meant to remain as minnows forever?"

Balancing stick in Man's tightrope walk to destiny

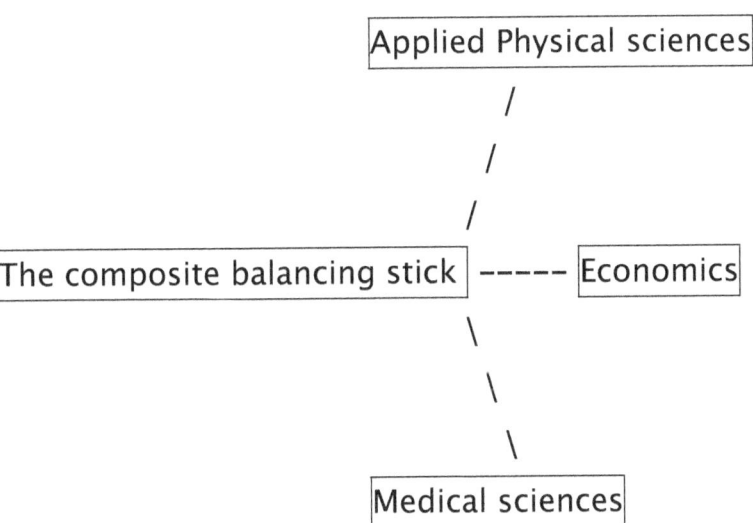

As Economics is part of the composite balancing lever it can be easy accepted that it has a role in human welfare like the other sciences. Welfare starts with facing the poser and answering it.

Pundits engaged in the discipline of Economics will not agree though. They are in the practice of offloading the extremely obnoxious issue by referring it to a breed of their sidekicks – the politicians – who owe their existence to Economic pundits because the latter are extremely reluctant to take the big question.

Economists cannot allow the poser to get into active play. They dodge it rather easily by not choosing to start Economics with anything that resembles total welfare of all humans – that is, the human-end of it –but start with the material-end and thereafter making it so prodigiously elaborate, fractured and disjointed that by the time one finishes with the subject one hardly remembers what the subject is about except for some irascible entities like Money, Market and the like.

This book does not accept the ruse that this question does not come under the purview of Economics.

The reason is simple. An area of intellectual pursuit whose trademark is evasiveness cannot claim itself to be a science of any sort, physical or else. Even the huge quantum of erudite involvement and enormous volume of data gleaned from real-life cannot prevent the subject from sounding hollow. Such a contrived subject loses credibility and reliability. The impressive array of Nobel laureates associated with the subject only helps it gain verisimilitude at best.

Welfare and welfare scheme are not synonymous. In order to gain universal acceptability Economics must earnestly focus on welfare of all human beings, not merely a tiny section of it and that too at the expense of the huge majority. Applying the balm of welfare schemes on deprived humanity as an afterthought after stabbing them with ruthless marketeering weapons is a ruse verging on skullduggery.

The main trunk of Economics is conspicuous by its studied silence of human welfare. That the poor is poor and will remain poor while poverty will deepen and widen endlessly has much to do with endorsement by Economics of predatorial Market practices

The Market has players of all hues, all statures and all attitudes. All those who have products to sell participate in the Market. They either sell that is, simply offer their products on sale to prospective buyers and negotiate a rate with them to arrive at a deal, else, promote their products along with the offer of sale which we may call marketing.

Pigeons are gentle, gregarious and generally peace-loving creatures who are easy target of the prowling predator, particularly when they are idling.

The mass that is, bulk of the populace come under the category of pigeons. They are a cluster of unambitious, unimaginative and unmotivated people whose probable emergence as buyers is blocked by low income.

The great dilemma that Capitalism faces is that the gain that the big boys make by outsmarting the minnows works as a self-deprivation inasmuch as the prospective buyers of their products are lost. The bright boys of Capitalism are bright because the dull boys are dull.

Contrasting ways of approaching the buyer

The average man

Selling --→-----\   /--→------Deal
          \   /
    direct\   /
  product offer\   /
     \ /
    Rate fixing ----<-------Buyer
     /   /
    /   indirect/
 product offer/   influence/
   /   /
Marketing --→--/--→---------------/

The privileged man

It is not hard to at all why Economics fosters despair among the average people. Every average person since birth has been seeing the face of despair staring at him sphinx like that very often goes on lasting lifelong. For so long and with such intensity the stare continues that these people forget to even dream of a decent prosperous life. With its perverted approach that supports the mighty and truculent protagonists of dominance through Market machinations, Economics does its deadly best to ensure that this deathly glare of despair on the average man remains unabated throughout the world, throughout eons of time.

Fortunately, Economics is not the Holy Book, contents of which are not unquestionable, unimpeachable or unchangeable. So, hope is there certainly for the hapless average mass, only it has to be given shape.

The defining moment when the average man loses out to the privileged man is during fixing of the relative selling rates of their products. The naïve average man can make only a direct offer while the crafty privileged man has many tricks up his sleeve to clinch a far better deal. Thus, rate is not fixed by utility of a product but the calculated drama that goes in its selling process.

Market rivalry

```
                              producers–cum–sellers
                             /
                            /
                   Criers --- small, numerous
                  /     \
                 /       \
                /         no marketing      traders
               /                           /
              /                           /
Buyer's attention seekers --------- Triers --- ad
            \                             \
             \                             \
              \          service            traditional
               \        /
                \      /
                Viers --- technology/ IT combined
                     \
                      \
                      modern
```

The selling process involves essentially three types of sellers namely, the Criers, the Triers and the Viers. Criers are the permanent losers – toiling, unimaginative and unpretentious. They do not know how to earn the most from their products when they put their products in the transactions–cauldron. The rates–potion that they are able to catch hold of is abysmally poor as a result.

Thus, they are the lay pigeons. They are the clay pigeons as well, presenting themselves as easy objects for target practice of brilliant Economists.

Parables of the Market Partakers

 Chapter ~ 7 ~

The Partaker equations

Market is the traditional arena where chalks are exchanged against cheese in ratios that nobody determines yet everybody follows. It has since transcended its humble material antecedents to become an abstraction with powers of a demigod but without material existence. As such, Market decides Rates of Exchange (RoE) but cannot take questions regarding how and why of such decisions, being a conveniently notional entity.

A = Seller of chalk, Buyer of cheese

```
        x kg                    y kg
 chalk -→--\              /-→-- cheese
            \            /
         Rate of Exchange
            /            \
 cheese -→--/              \-->-- chalk
        y kg                    x kg
```

B = Seller of cheese, Buyer of chalk

Absolute Rate of Exchange (R_0) = (y / x).

R is as arbitrary as chalk is dissimilar to cheese. Let us replace chalk with medicine and cheese with food to get behind the curtain.

A = Seller of food, Buyer of medicine

B = Seller of medicine, Buyer of food

Absolute Rate of Exchange $(R_0) = (y / x)$ ml/kg.

A grows wheat in his field with crude implements while B manufactures medicine in his laboratory with sophisticated equipment and technology.

As both the items are essential to life it boils down to capability of the seller to resist selling pressure. A, the tiny agriculturist, does not have adequate and proper space to hold on to his stock and wait for better rates. Moreover, some items like vegetable and fish are rapidly perishable. Also, being an unorganized individual, his reach in the network is severely limited. He is keen to sell off at the earliest. M_0, the traditional middleman, has storage space as well as network at points-of-sale and buys the stock at a cheap rate.

Power and space expenses make cost of storage on a prolonged basis a big load even on the wealthy M_0. There are no such issues with B, the Big Businessman, since these contingent costs are aptly provided for while setting his margin. Taking n as **n**eed, s as **s**carcity and c as **c**ost

$$P_0 = c + J_0 / c + J_1 . n . s \quad [J, J_0, J_1, J_2 \text{ constant}$$
$$= c + J_0 / c + J . n^2 \quad [s = J_2 . n, J = J_1 . J_2$$

where P_0, the Absolute Rate Earning Potential (AREP), is more need-sensitive than it is cost-sensitive.

Now, P_0 needs moderation by factoring in of Bargaining Handicap (h) and the consequent Operational Hazard (h_1), proportional to h, with more hurdles for food than for medicine. The Absolute Rate of Exchange R_0 is

$$R_0 = P_0 . [(K . a) - L_0 . (h . h_1)] = P_0 . [(K . a) - (L . h^2)]$$

where a is the accentuation factor related to Concerted Persistent Marketing Efforts (CPME). Against the neutral scale of Money, we get the Rationalized Rate of Exchange (R) that is, the rate a product fetches as

$$
\begin{aligned}
R &= R_0 . s . t \\
&= P_0 . s . t . [(K . a) - (L . h^2)] \\
&= s . t . [c + (J_0 / c) + (J . n^2)] . [(K . a) - (L . h^2)]
\end{aligned}
$$

where s is seasonal urge and t is temptation linked to buyer's Taste, Penchant, Liquidity, Spree and Mood.

This Base Equation of Rate is not meant to compute RoE theoretically since the pillars on which it stands namely, constants J_0, J, K and L are entirely unknown. It serves an important purpose though – that is of revealing the interrelation among the variables in it.

For mundane requirements of life that also have low cost of production such as cereals c, a, s and t – all have the attributed base value of 1. So, for basic items

$$R_b = [1 + J_0 + (J \cdot n^2)] \cdot [K - (L \cdot h^2)]$$

that is, R_b is highly sensitive of fluctuation in n and h.

Arguably, the relative values of J_0, J, K and L would vary from product to product. Consequently, relative impact of changes in c, h, a, n t and s (chants) may be widely different although there is a common feature in these that all of these are susceptible to control.

More comprehensively a competitor can wield control over chant the more successful he can be among peers in the Market. But when it is a tussle between chalk and cheese such control may not mean much. Here the role of **c, a** and **t (cat)** becomes highly significant since n and h are of little consequence for non–essential items and s has an irregular impact. How the big cat, the predator, goes about hunting its prey is the key to understanding the myth of the Market.

The cat can grab attention and divert resources of the buyer away from essential items such as food to non-essential items such as fashion and entertainment. The poor agriculturist A lacks the dauntlessness of the doughty **mouse** (**m**eans, **o**rganization, **u**nderstanding, **s**kill or **e**ndurance) in him that can bell the cat. In fact, he cannot control RoE at all. He just capitulates.

The new-generation Intermediary (middleman), I, is vastly superior to I_0 and has a cat of his own. He unleashes his cat among pigeons – the traditional I_0s.

In fact, there are two parallel Market-Types. One, the Traditional Market-Old (M_0), free of cat and embracing old practices where seller has a direct, real interface with buyer. Here products presented for sale, has RoE arrived at through the process of auction at individual level. Two, the Modern Market-New (M_1) with upscale ambience and mindsets where cats fight out bloody battles for gaining advantage in RoE.

Each Market-Type has two Market-Modes under it. Thus, we get four Market-Modes in all namely, M_0a, M_0b, M_1a and M_1b. While these Market-Modes vie with one another for space the cat moves in to play meddler.

Markets and their Essential Characters

Moneyless seller–buyer–interface

/ **Mode–0a** : barter of goods

Type–0 /

Traditional no cat

/ \

/ \

/ Direct seller–buyer–interface

/ **Mode–0b** : goods for cash

Market Types

\

\ Seductive–appeal approach

\ / **Mode–1a** : hype marketeering

\ /

Modern ruled by cat

Type–1 \

\

Mesmeric–bully approach

Mode–1b : sync marketeering

Slowly but surely, M_1 captures space displacing M_0 with its appeal of sophistication, particularly strongly when the subject is young.

Animal instinct of the cat is the telling feature of modernity in Market, only the cat does not toil. It is a bully and an opportunist that also steals toil of others – millions who sweat it out at fields braving blistering sun and torrential rain.

The big cat, a gregarious animal, also hunts in hordes. The cat actually lives in a cartel, which can be described as the acronym of

c = cut-throat

a = aggressive

r = ruthless

t = threatening

e = encroaching

l = libertarian.

It not only fights its own battle but also that of the cartel in defending M_1 against M_0. It is an unprovoked one-sided running battle in a turf war for capturing territory with the aim of making RoE level of M_1 abnormally higher than that of M_0. It ensures that buyers' total resources are captured more by M_1 at the expense of M_0. The *modus operandi* resembles Vietnam and Indonesia of the last Sixties in many of its critical aspects in the aftermath of which Vietnam stood up to the challenge and Indonesia capitulated and suffered a puppet dictator for half-a-century.

This is the way the RoE works out between chalk and cheese in the Market with the fierce marauding cat lurking somewhere in-between and pawing subtly.

In the final count, M_1 – populated by a few participants and select patrons – take away the lion's share of the resources available for change of hands while M_0 – with participation of teeming millions always struggling for survival – lose out badly.

This is the Market mechanism of fixing RoE – objective, impartial and fair on the surface but the deeper you dig into it the more diabolical, fierce and hideous it looks.

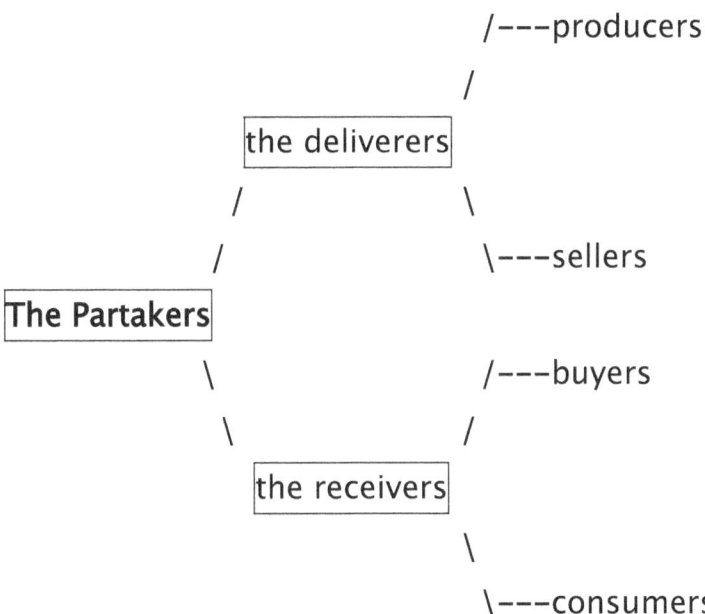

Many among these teeming millions survive but barely. Many have only a single meal per day, many do not even have that regularly. People die of starvation too or commit suicide when unable to cope with the prospect of imprisonment for failing to pay back loans.

This is the usual scenario that becomes even more cruel in times of crop failure because of drought or flood. These people have nothing to fall back on at times of distress. The ruthless Market leaves them with no savings. The Market is, in fact, a euphemism for organized and dressed up racket.

This is a despairing scenario, particularly in India. Vast majority of Indian people figures in the average mass – the object of abomination of the privileged few although the latter are not necessarily superior humans on the count of innate quality. The net result is that the country remains poor because the majority of its populace is poverty–stricken.

Only buyers can set right the skewed propriety in the rate–fixing scenario. Only if buyers refuse to pay fancy prices for non–essential items the rates gap will reduce to reasonable levels giving the scenario a humane turn.

Such starvation deaths happen in India too – a country that produces enough food for full sustenance of its entire populace. It is a cruel irony but it never seems to bother the Economists.

The reason is simple enough. The Market, dominated by M_1, rob them in association with their conduit, the Intermediary I_0, of their dues by siphoning off buyers' resources more to the cartel than the cartel deserves.

Parables of the Market Partakers

CHAPTER ~ 8 ~

Fat cat dithyramb

The liberty that came with introduction of *laissez faire* was highly rewarding to some and extremely regressive to most. Over centuries *laissez faire* has been able to create and harden a mindset that makes it widely acceptable. It has come to occupy the position of the Holy Book of World Religion with the Market as its God. The fact is, *laissez faire* has outlived its use.

Fairness – the highest attribute of *laissez faire* that used to separate it from other forms of trade practices in the early days of its advent has undergone such a degree of mutation that it is untraceable today except in its indelible persistence in the name itself.

When chalk and cheese are brought into the Market for trading the seller of chalk may not be hungry for cheese and the seller of cheese may also not be interested in use of chalk. In fact, it is more unlikely than not to find a reciprocal relation existing between the two. Yet either is tagged with a rate of exchange in terms of Money. It looks like a paradox but actually it is not. It becomes easier to see through the paradox if we take into account the Zing (z) aspect besides the utility (affordability, necessity ((need, scarcity)) and ware (cost, handicap (hazards, hurdles)) aspects.

The Zing factor (z) gives the product a countenance. Where ability to fetch high price is concerned, other factors pale into insignificance compared to z in the matter of relative weightage. As such,

$$F = S . T . (X . u + (Y / w) + z) \quad [X, Y \text{ constant}$$

where F is Fetchable Rate of Exchange (FRoE) and, usually, we find z > (X . u) as also z > (Y / w), u=utility aspect, w=ware aspect, S=Supermarketeer Syndrome that gains superiority by tactically stifling cross–Market rivalry and T=toning of buyers' minds by tinting, tempting, and tampering. Value Magnification (V) is a composite quantity made up of T and z. For items having relatively low u and w with z >> (X . u) and z >> (Y / w) we arrive at the approximation

$$F = S . T . z = S . V \qquad [V = T . z.$$

Items such as cosmetics, games and fashion–attire coming under this category have few cross–Market rivals to deal with but where heavy investment in T and z is grotesquely evident, inevitable and unreconcilable with sanity from a poor's priority point of view (PPP).

F is the quantity that determines relative RoE of products in the Market.

That T and z are facts of life – from which there is apparently no escape – is hard to accept for many, particularly those minds who are given to weighing options with rationalization in every sphere of life. Not that all of those people are too rigidly conventional or averse to the lighter side of life. They are mostly principled people whose aversion is directed at the motive with which dirty minds – mostly undeserving – engage themselves in plundering the fruits of toil and endless drudgery of the ignorant multitude by using the handle of the Market.

Now z is dependent on various forms of gimmickry the most potent of which is advertisement. As ads are nowadays boosted by technology and professional mind–play in media presentation, sellers tend to spend huge amounts on these.

The buyer of a product gets lots of frills loaded onto it. Frill is zing that would not sell unless accompanying the product. Eateries with expensive ambience is a case in point. There are no takers for the ambience exclusive of the food. Consumers do not object to the incongruously high rate of food as they are mentally conditioned and toned to accept such incongruity.

The cat is a creature of *laissez faire* and a mindless predator adept in the use of teeth and claws on others. Sadly, even predators have the right to life unless they are given to deliberate killings on occasions that do not warrant extreme measures for defending oneself against actual attack.

So, the cat lives on with aplomb – roaming, rampaging and ruining millions of lives. It roves about with impunity and extends its hunting zone continuously with time in geometrical proportions. It keeps a wary eye on the prospects and changes that might be in the offing. It is wily, it does not rush things but systematically wears down the opponent with its SICK (Sustained and Intense Campaign to Kill) strategy.

Everything that it does is highly legitimate as it is perfectly in line with the tenets of *laissez faire*. Actually, the malady lies in *laissez faire* itself.

In the early days of *laissez faire* when the level of technology was not much different from the primitive *laissez faire* played a very progressive and constructive role and, in many ways, was instrumental in organizing resistance against rule of tyranny by the bully.

Technology – introduced in course of the Industrial Revolution and, with the help of scientific research, having a phenomenal flourish with rapid reinvention ever since – not only changed the face of the production mode and the product – adding new dimensions to the product – but also transformed the way the Market used to be run.

An example should make it amply clear. Let us take the case of hired passenger road transport in India or, if we may, the specific instance of the city of Kolkata. The air here has a laid–back smell with millions thronging the inadequate roads in daytime on a business day. Roads are congested so are the pavements. Even as hundreds of thousands of yellow taxis ply here the modern–age internet–powered white taxis have been doing brisk business ever since these came into the picture some six years back, using similar Indian vehicle brands and drivers. The product here is the all too familiar problem–ridden yet essential transport service, buyers or users of which are the same local people yet the white taxis come as fresh entrants and win away a large chunk of the Market–share despite there being no dearth of traditional yellow taxis.

This phenomenon is an eye-opener for the existence of parallel Market-Types M_0 and M_1. It worked like magic in a segment where the sellers are fleet-owners with traditional mindset employing drivers to operate the yellow taxis (YT) on one hand and affluent up-and-coming businessmen - rank outsiders - leasing white taxis (WT) from owner-drivers. While YT - without air-conditioning - pick up passengers at the taxi stand WT - always air-conditioned - on receiving booking through internet pick them up right at their doorsteps. WT make huge profits because first, they are able to put their fleet of cabs to optimal usage and secondly, although suave, they can be really unfriendly and cut-throat when availability of service is scarce as they never hesitate to raise their variable rates wildly. In the first case - of YT - Market functions in traditional M_0 mode while WT trades in modern Market M_1.

Actually, there is no competition between YT and WT because they operate in different, parallel Markets. Moreover, the core service is transportation that both YT and WT provide. WT wins its customers not with its core service but with its added services - comfort, convenience and civility.

While role of quality of added service is enormous in this case, the clinching issue here is the use of technology which, being the enabler of efficient and quality added service, kills the competition.

With remarkable ease WT neatly sidestepped the issue of competition with homegrown operators of YT. WT just invoked an uneven playing field. They operated from a height to which YT had no access because of their antiquated style made up with stale and directionless power lobbies, ingrained customs hardened with time and comfort in the quagmire of laidback attitudes to which millions subscribed.

This is the stark reality. The running warfare is between two parallel Markets M_0 and M_1 solely. The seller-subscribers to M_0 namely M_{0in} (M_{0a1}, M_{0a2}, M_{0b1}, M_{0b2} etc) do compete among themselves while at the same time unite to take up the cudgels under the flag of M_0. Similarly, seller-subscribers to M_1 namely M_{1in} (M_{1a1}, M_{1a2}, M_{1b1}, M_{1b2} etc) despite competing among themselves unite to fight for the interest of M_1.

There is no tussle for supremacy between a seller-subscriber to M_0 e.g., M_{0a1} and another to M_1 e.g., M_{1b2}.

One more instance – a story from Indian mythology. The Ramayana reaches its climax in the epic war between the armies of Rama and Ravana over the island of Lanka. During height of war, Ravana's son Indrajit rides up to the clouds and shoots deadly arrows at Rama's army from behind the clouds. Rama's brother Lakshman is seriously injured by one such arrow.

The story underlines lack of fairness in competition. Nobody finds fault with the battlefield manners of Indrajit because all he did was to make use of a vara – an empowerment – he had received from Lord Indra earlier that gave him such advantage. It was a stealthy, cowardly and unprincipled act nevertheless. Despite it not being a level playing field, nobody could raise a finger against Indrajit as he played by the book. The discretion of the recipient – the veera – to use the vara on the occasion was thought to be well within the presumed limits of veeratwa – code of conduct of the courageous warrior – even in those days of truthfulness, godliness and chivalry. The effect might be nastily outrageous but none complained. Answer to such legitimate chicanery lies in being stubborn, tough and unconventional. Not in sportsmanship but in gamesmanship.

Modern history is also replete with similar instances – analogy becomes apparent if looked at objectively.

USA brought on its floating stationed fleet a huge arsenal of sophisticated weaponry with capability of mass destruction to Indo-China in mid–last–century, soon after dropping of atom bomb on Japan to end World War II and buoyed by that success. Reaction to the maddening fear of rapidly spreading communism, the war was unilateral, unprovoked and utterly unethical. The poor peasants of Indo-China were stunned. That they did not capitulate is one of the greatest real stories in the history of chivalry.

It is said that nothing is unfair in love and war. When it is conflict arising out of resistance to defend homeland against aggression by a bully from outside who has no business to be there in that homeland it should be called var (vile aggression and resistance). The adage that relates to war not necessarily applies to var.

The ulterior motive behind such apparently wild act lies in the fact that unless the extant Market M_0 at those lands get converted to M the ever–growing volumes of products manufactured at USA and other Capitalist countries would soon run out of takers in the world.

It was a patently and brutally uneven playing field. Aiming to establish their deviant Market clockwork on those lands USA dropped napalm bombs on children, eliminated hundreds of thousands of peasants in the space of a week and dug massive pits to act as mass grave to bury them. Their puppet – the mastermind of this genocide – became Head of the State – a state that swung between autocracy and sham democracy – holding on to power unto death decades later.

Even after all these they talk of Hitler with pretended hatred to establish the insane untruth that they are different from Hitler. That their dastardly acts in Indo-China was prompted by saintly objectives.

It is a wonder that people of USA – conscientious as they are – do not think differently. Had they done so the admirers of those characters – whose bloody hands carried out the boorish acts - would hardly find their idols' pictures hanging in public places without the slightest reaction from people at large in the form of condemnation, disparagement or even mild exclamation. Yet they hold strong opinions about society, nation and the world. They see a lot, talk even more but do not speak out at all to call a spade a spade.

The world is travelling in time towards a destination where animals rule. Hemingway remains only on the cover of books since going through the distance between the cover and the contents is too hard a mental toil for most people to actually do who are treading the present-day stage and heading for the unlived future. People - including the intellectually gifted among them - are inclined to buy luxury of listless living casting aside the doughnuts of dreary drudgery.

Unless lessons are taken from History, there is no point in studying History. The part involving application in thought process through self-education with its culmination in formation of a life-philosophy is largely missing. Dead minds, characteristics of those leading lives full of staid, untroubled luxury have the life-philosophy of evasive convenience to go with which is poor substitute for the vibrant, exponentially self-surpassing life-philosophy. Luxury as killer of mind's initiatives can be worse than what drudgery is thought to be. Sadly, reading and studying have come to be regarded as more synonymous than they had ever been.

Parables of the Market Partakers

CHAPTER ~ 9 ~

A cat by its tail

Patently, magic of the modern Market emerges from subtle adaptation of tactical finesse coupled with technological in selling operations which is an aspect that complements the product itself. This magic or, v (Value Magnification by Coupling of Operations and Features) is the ratio of F against R (F/R).

So, we have,

$$F = S . T . (X . u + (Y / s) + z) = S . T . z \text{ (app)}$$

$$R = s . t . [c + (J_0 / c) + (J . n^2)] . [(K . a) - (L . h^2)]$$

$$v = (S.T/s.t).z/[(c + (J_0 / c) + (J . n^2)) . ((K . a) - (L . h^2))].$$

Or, $v = S_i . T_i . z_i$ [$s_i = S / s$, $T_i = T / t$, $z_i = z / [..]$.

While Toning (T) works deep by morphing the buyer's mind Temptation (t) is superficial and merely pampers. So, T is more potent than t making T_i highly positive.

Zing (z) covers the social aspect to make z_i positive. Evidence of this lies in the example of the mobile phone. Even poor people who can ill-afford minimum nutrition in their food go for mobile phones. Here cost (c), need (n), accentuation (a) and handicap (h) are no match for Zing, a combination of convenience, lifestyle and demonstrative values of the product.

Finally, it is the quantity S_i that needs clarification at length. S, the Super-marketeer Syndrome, is basically two-pronged Market maneuvering by application of technology firstly for plain operational prowess and secondly to innovate processes – so powerfully yet delicately crafted with software and networking that when it fails the system collapses as the entire gamut of processes are rendered non-functional – to outwit, stifle and crush rivals so that competition becomes insignificant and one-sided. The strategy rides on the fact that rivals cannot afford such delicacy. As such, s is a weak response compared to S when Market invites.

Towards this, methodical deployment of strategy and technology is of immense import as explained under. One, a parallel Supermarket is created where access to high technology is essential prerequisite. Two, this requires large-scale funding so that those who are not savvy with such technology or not adequately endowed with funds are left out of the race summarily. Three, buyers – particularly young aspiring people – are courted in innovative ways to leave lasting impression that in turn inspire curiosity, confidence and cult following. A seller not given to innovative ways is bound to be a non-starter.

There is always a limited amount of buyer's buying power available and up for grabbing. How does the buyer spend it and in what proportions depend on the buyer's mental balance as well as the seller's acumen, initiative and ability to induce changes in the buyer's mental balance in seller's favour. Once this is accomplished and the buyer is half-committed the seller sets his price. The seller of chalk may extract ten times the rate of seller of cheese depending on the relative degree of his own accomplishment.

So, relative rates may be projected as

B = Rate of chalk/ Rate of cheese

= Relative importance of chalk and cheese *

(Convincing power of seller of chalk/

Convincing power of seller of cheese)

where B is the bias of the buyer and the basis of his spending pattern. It is a complex of the internal factor of his preformed notion of relative importance of chalk and cheese and imposed factor of how sellers are able to convince him. Bias translates to actual quantum and direction of spending by the buyer that fixes the rates.

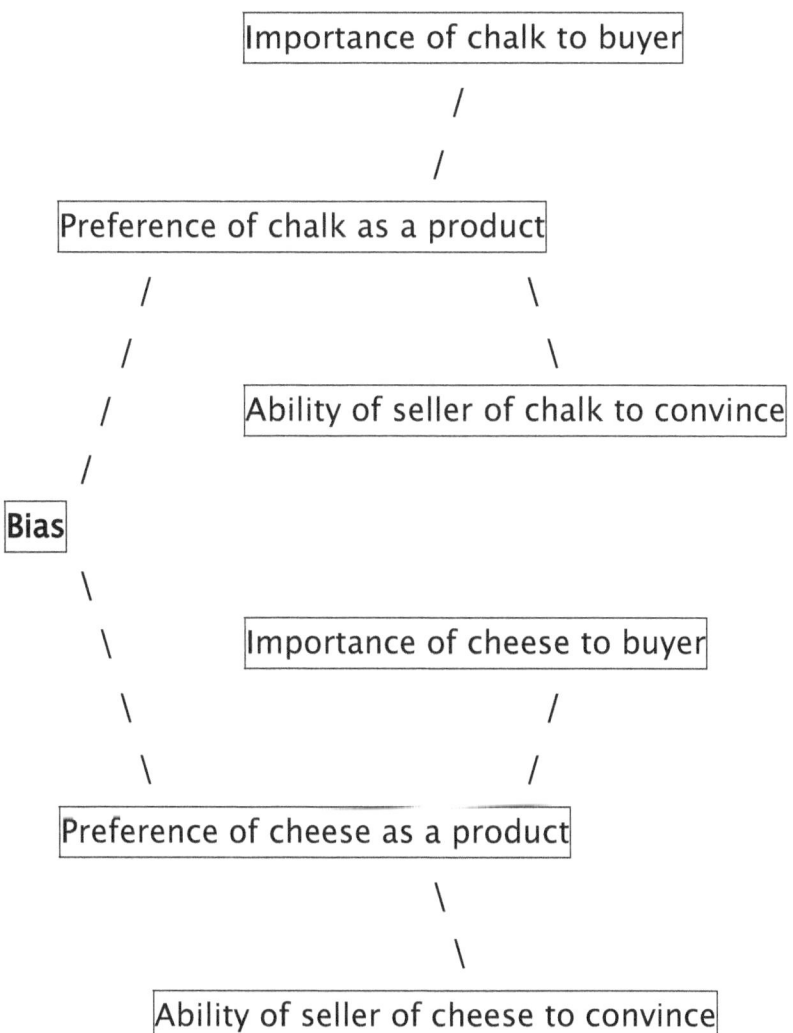

B may be related to Market as $B = r \cdot T \cdot z$

where r is buyer's Receptivity to conditioning.

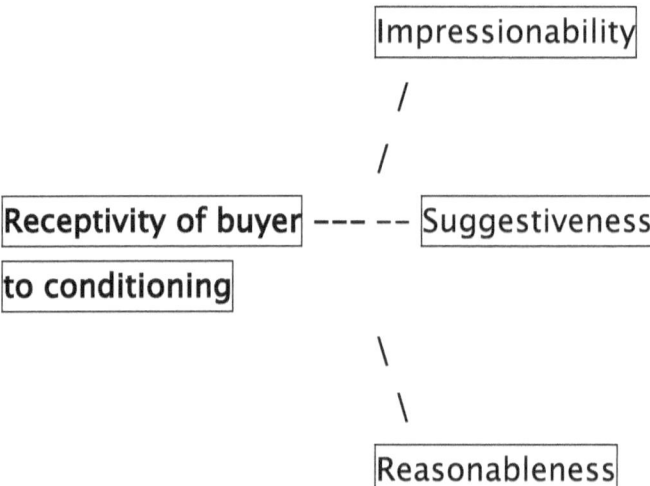

It is extremely unlikely that all three attributes of the mind are equally strongly active in an individual's mind or work in tandem simultaneously in the mind. The relative measures may vary widely person to person. To average people – who matter most in Market play – Impressionability has the greatest say. To fine people suggestibility works fine. To the hard-nosed, Reasonableness has no substitute. In fact, some stimulus that may stir the Impressionability cells of the mind may turn the Reasonableness cells of the same person violently against the stimulus or, *vice versa*.

Since a very overwhelmingly large section of the people around the world have in them Impressionability as the dominant trait it will be prudent to go after this trait without bothering to be suggestive or reasonable. This would be the smartest way to win control the average buyer's Bias. That is what Receptivity (r) is all about.

It needs tact to make arouse buyers' Receptivity. Approaches relying on Suggestiveness or Reasonableness have their limitations as the takers are fewer in number. Grabbing the Market is after all a number game.

Now, $F = S . T . z$

$\qquad B = r . T . z.$

So, $\quad F / B = S / r = Q$

$\qquad$ or, $F = B . Q.$

Quantizability (Q) is the ability of the seller to crystallize his Bias advantage to rate advantage through Super-marketeering (S).

Obstacles facing lay–pigeons sellers to grab rightful share of buyers' spendings are threefold namely, (1)plain product, (2)Bias and (3)Super–marketeering.

Marketing issues faced by lay-pigeon sellers

Product plainness
/ self-aspect
/
/
Marketing obstacles -------- Buyer Bias
\ buyer-aspect
\
\
Super-marketeering
Competitor-aspect

The first one, plainness of product is the self-aspect of the seller. The second one, Bias, is the buyer-aspect. The third one, Super-marketeering, is the competitor-aspect.

Basic products that lay-pigeon sellers deal with like foodgrain, vegetable, oil, fish, meat, egg, dairy items, fruits, salt, sugar, cotton, jute, silk, timber, bamboo, lac, medicinal plants etc are not easily glorifiable.

Moreover, being naïve, illiterate and unorganized are enormous handicaps against sharp, ruthless and well-funded opponents in the Market. The smell of opportunity in the form of (1)a rapidly growing Economy that hands more and more spending power to the buyer (2)more relaxed lending by financial institutions (3)vast Indian Market, much of which is untapped (4)highly underprepared sellers. The smell draws in the sharks equipped with their Super-marketeering teeth. They do not vie with the lay-pigeons for space in Competition but just drink the blood of Competition that is, spending power of the buyer.

So, however flushed the Market may be with buyers' spending power the root-level producers of basic items who are condemned to abject poverty since time immemorial will remain so unless they think out-of-box to devise strategy that makes the sharks sterile.

Before we look at the elements of a possible strategy, we take a more intense look at Competition as it exists now. Let us think of Competition as embodied in a feminine form.

Modus operandi of competitors in Market

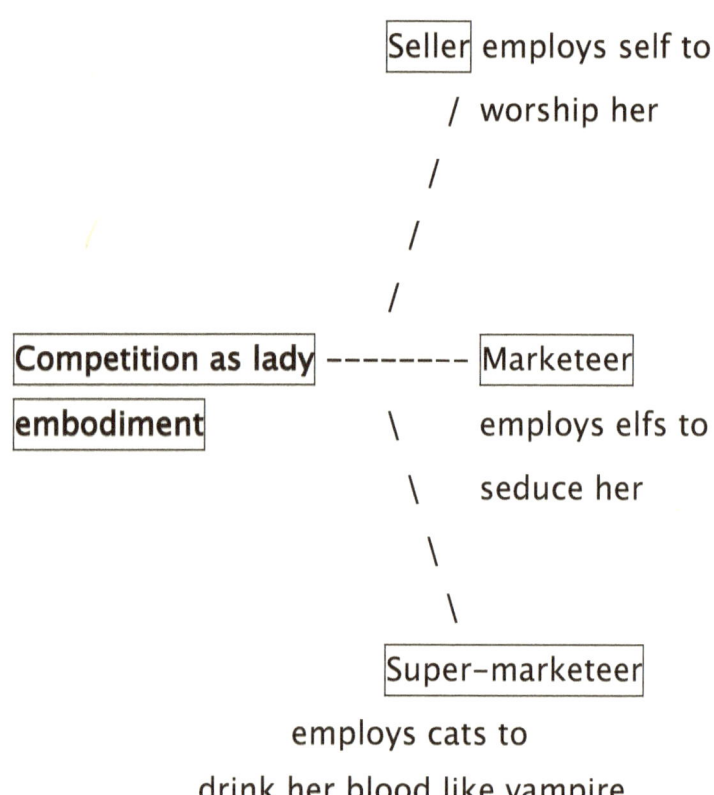

Seller employs self to
/ worship her
/
/
/
Competition as lady ──────── Marketeer

embodiment   \   employs elfs to

                     \   seduce her

                      \

                       \

Super-marketeer

employs cats to

drink her blood like vampire

The Seller or, the naïve lay–pigeon seller does not do any marketing – not bothering to take pains to make his product appear more acceptable in the Market – apart from bringing his ware to the Market or to the Intermediaries I_0 and I.

The Marketeer markets his products by going all–out to add charms of different varieties – elfs we may call those – to the product to enhance the attractiveness of the product.

The Super–marketeer is hell–bent on grabbing his pound of flesh by tweaking the very process of marketing – as if genetically transforming the process – with the help of technology that is, software and networking.

As the charmless and artless Seller can neither hold attraction for the essentially Impressionable buyer nor afford extravagantly elaborate machinations to undermine the traditional Market by putting a parallel Market in place, he has to look for other choices. He needs to strike at the very root of the phenomenon that the Market is and tweak notions about the Market.

Strategic solutions for the beleaguered Seller

1 need not cater

/ to buyer's

/ Impressionability

/

/

Seller's strategy elements ---- 2

\ need not indulge

\ in machinations

\

\

3

Push rates up for his own products

by making the products scarce

The Seller's ultimate aim is to capture the majority of buyers' spending power and he cannot remain complacent with some rise in the rate that does not translate to significant rise in share or the share may even decline.

One way of making the products – mostly essential for survival – scarce is to hold on to them for a sufficiently long time. It needs Govt support and infrastructure such as storage space – particularly, cold storage. Govt support may come in the form of high tariff barriers to imports of similar goods into the Market. Govt may also impose extremely high sales taxes on local open-market sales of these articles except when sold to through co-operatives or Govt arms who would take the responsibility of selling the products in the wholesale Market. The sales tax revenue so earned by Govt may be used to fund a free-food-for-every-poor project. Since only cooked food is to be distributed free among enlisted poor whose biometric identity are pre-recorded, chances of corruption are minimized. Such a project could conceivably create millions of jobs for youngsters who have some education and basic computer handling knowledge.

Seller's withdrawal strategy Review–A

/   1 compulsion

/   on the buyer to

/   spend more on

/   need–items

/

/

Prongs' blueprint ---- 2

\   less spending on weed–items

\   like shares, gambling, car,

\   fashion, alcohol, real–estate,

\ art, jewelry, entertainment

\

\   3

less availability of buyers'
spending–power makes huge
investment on technology
unviable and pre–empts/ foils
Super–marketeering forays

Seller's withdrawal strategy Review-B

$$/ \quad \boxed{1}$$

/   forced scarcity

/   leads to much higher

/   rates for need–items

/   in open Market at the

/   expense of weed–items

/

Direct benefits ------- $\boxed{2}$

\   every poor gets one

\   free meal every day in

\   cooked form

\

\

\ $\boxed{3}$

millions of jobs are

created in running

free–kitchens

Seller's withdrawal strategy Review–C

/   1

/   concentration pattern

/   of spending–power of

/   buyer shifts to working

/   people from parasites

/

/

Economic impacts ---- 2

\   interest shifts from

\   food to other less

\   dire consumptions

\   like bare housing, child

\   health, education etc

\

\   3

inflation rises but poor

is unhurt, growth is

unabated sans

gimmickry

Seller's withdrawal strategy Review–D

/   1

/   parasites without merit

/   linked to marketeering

/   /Super-marketeering

/   get more and more

/   irrelevant

/

Social impacts ------- 2

\   social disparity shrinks

\   as economic equality

\   gets foothold, casting

\   aside obscure norms of

\   cast/religion

\

\   3

vicious pools such as

gambling, speculating,

trafficking lose steam

as idle funds dry up

Seller's withdrawal strategy Review–E

```
                    /      1
                   /           deprived of free food
                  /            benefit and has to buy
                 /             food at sky-high prices
                /
               /
Middle class quandary  ------ 2
                \              needs to cut expenses
                 \             on frills and tiny luxury
                  \            items like expensive
                   \           flat, car, foreign travel
                    \
                     \     3
                               pressurizes foreign
                               capital to hike wages
                               leading to further rise
                               in inflation
```

Inflation need not be a deterrent in this plan because the benefits that accrue from gains of inflation go to the poor in the form of free meals. The rich and even the not-so-rich have enough resources of their own to take care of themselves. A country with 80% people living under abject poverty should neither shed tears for the rich and the super-rich nor get its priorities fixed by them.

Eventually, it is more a matter of political will than of financial acumen to put such a plan into action. It is very difficult to expect such a radical recipe from the political class who liaise intimately with the Marketeers and Super-marketeers – the latter mostly with close links with foreign capital – and actually owe their allegiance to them. They exhibit their cultivated closeness to the Sellers only when the occasion comes for capturing democratic powers. Sellers have the numbers that really matter in democracy but they are only offered a choice between the devil and the deep sea. Democracy rotates by the torque created by such contestants while constructive forces are forced out of the contest by suppressing them with uninhibited use of brawn, bullets and brutality to deadly effect.

It transpires that technology is the tail of the cat that every pigeon should be wary of. Tail is where aggressive intent finds its most emphatic expression. As the cat whips up its tail in the air and simultaneously rents the air with its typically harsh war cry with its claws and teeth in the attacking mode the belligerence can hardly remain unnoticed.

Confronting the cat head-on in such mood can only court trouble. It is poor strategy if getting the better of the cat is your aim. Show of valour does not mean much if you do not live to see the valour earned you accolades from your fellow people and saved many of them from their terrible and untimely end in the hand of the cat. Bigger the cat, severer the injury by mauling. Very big cats, of course, can eat you up.

Technology is more misused than it is employed in the welfare of mankind.

Getting the better of the cat is absolutely essential to survival of sufferers yet the tough shield of legitimacy worn by the cat can foil any budding attempt to eliminate it or, at least, confine it in cage.

Parables of the Market Partakers

CHAPTER ~ 10 ~

Tailspin

At its core, the complex Capitalist System has a rather simple guiding spirit – to increase Capacity.

Capacity as the central theme of Capitalist System

```
                          producing
                           /
                          /
                         /
Increase Capacity of ------------------- selling
                         \
                          \
                           \
                          buying
```

Shift in Critical areas for Capitalists over time

     Phase-I (200–100 yrs back)

     production

      /

      /

    /Phase-II (100–50 yrs back)

Critical area –––––––––––––– selling

     \

      \

      \Phase-III (50 yrs back till now)

    buying

The scenario has been changing inexorably over the past two hundred years in sync with development of Capitalism. In the early days that is, Phase–I, production capacity was the prime focus as machines were handcrafted then and their availability was not easy.

Capitalism underwent a paradigm shift thereafter when in Phase–II machines themselves started producing machines of mass production. Production capacity went into a high trajectory as a consequence but was yet to attain the critical mass. The frantic momentum in the expansion of the capacity to produce left selling capacity stranded way behind though. Hence the capacity to sell became the prime focus. The selling capacity bottleneck eased out gradually through betterment of two objective conditions. First, rampant colonization widened the physical delimitations of the Market with which huge populace of the uncapitalized countries entered the fold of buyership. Secondly, rapid rise in world population catapulted selling capacity to a great height and also put selling into the fast gear mode.

With attaining of the critical mass came Phase–III. While both production capacity and selling capacity went on increasing at furious speed a new problem surfaced. People who will buy the immensely enlarged volume and variety of products were not provided with enough power to buy. Thus, in the present scenario capacity to buy becomes the prime focus. Till the struggling Capitalist think–tank is able stitch together a solution, capacity to buy remains the prime focus.

It is pertinent to note that while in Phase–I and Phase–II the critical area did lie in their own domain Capitalists have now resolve a problem that is directly not their own. They cannot close their eyes on it though for obvious reasons. Thus, they are unwittingly trapped into doing the distasteful work of having to lift the have–nots from the morass of dire poverty and unemployment they are in – a work which they can neither put their heart to nor from which they can escape for the sake of saving their own system from certain disaster. It may be poetic justice it may be not but it is certain that Capitalists are finessed out to do what Equalites has been dreaming of for over centuries – since the advent of Capitalism to be precise.

In other words, opinion makers of various hues in the world have started converging towards a single view, albeit from different directions and with contrasting modalities. Approach of the Capitalists reminds one of the notorious quote from one of the principal protagonists in the French Revolution. What Marie Antoinette proposed for consumption of the starving populace – cake in lieu of bread – seems to have caught the imagination of the present-day Capitalists. Handsomely paid limited number of jobs are offered to highly educated, technically qualified or skilled people who are not average at all. Bread of the average person is lying at the same distance away from him as before.

The reason is, Capitalists are not prepared to cede an iota of space in the Market to the small producer–seller who form bulk of the average populace. They are ready to help out the poor with all other forms of assistance though. This contradiction in the attitude of Capitalists apparently verges on the puerile but actually here lies the crux of the Capitalist credo of "for the Market, of the Market and by the Market". Any softening of stand on the principle of ruthless Marketing sound self-defeating to them.

There seems to be no alternative in sight to the self-defeating medicine though. Thus, we expect to see the biggest climbdown in history, probably starting with a form of condescension.

A revelation that comes as a passing thought is that but a miniscule number of people are actually engaged in running the Capitalist machinery from sitting in their cozy perches. The rest of people associated with Capitalism are all hired hands and they form an impressive brigade. The really stunning part of it is that a very large majority of people are in fact have nothing to do with Capitalism at all. As such, it is not reasonable to accept Capitalism as the universal mantra without question.

At this point of time buyers are calling the shot everywhere although a large majority of the buyers are not indoctrinated in Capitalism and do not care to listen to its dogmatic compulsions. In fact, most of these people are so alienated from Capitalism for so long and with so much of bitterness that even a climbdown by the Capitalists may leave little impact on them. A climbdown may not be as easy as it seems.

The responsibility of bringing people unattached to Capitalism under the fold of Capitalism rests with none other than Capitalism itself nevertheless.

It is a moot point whether the Capitalists will be able to empower enough number of buyers with buying power before expansion of production capacity reaches such height that the system implodes for lack of adequate buyers.

The Big Time Bomb

```
very high production capacity becoming even higher
                  \
                   \
      ingredients of implosion  ---  impasse
                  /
                 /
very low per capita mass income becoming even lower
```

Economics does not answer questions of propriety, ethics and humanism. Such uncomfortable issues are carted off to other subjects one of which is Politics. Politics works as the faithful shield that stonewalls all such missiles directed at Economics. Politics does not answer such questions either but wears another shield called Democracy. By winning a Democratic election with majority of people's verdict in his favour a winner earns a moral reprieve additionally from not being able answer the questions of propriety.

It needs to be appreciated how Capitalism uses Politics – especially Democracy – for ulterior purposes. People's representatives do nothing to challenge the ruthlessness of Market. Both Capitalism and Democracy appear fair on paper as both are followers of apparently fair–play practices. Both survive because their respective subterfuges are not too obvious. The victims are the hapless mass in both cases.

When people get less and less impressed with their stated good intentions and shenanigans, out come the fangs and the claws. The Capitalism–Politics axis turn to armed intervention that would teach the non-conformers the right lesson that would last a long time.

The eventual winner will of course be man – not the selected few at the top – but the ocean of humanity.